# OPENING THE DOOR of FAITH

# OPENING THE DOOR of FAITH

*The Why, When, and Where of Evangelism*

John R. Hendrick

CTS PRESS
Decatur, Georgia

Unless otherwise indicated, Scripture quotations are from the *Revised Standard Version Bible,* copyright 1946, 1952, and © 1971 by the Division of Christian Education, National Council of the Churches of Christ in the U.S.A. and used by permission.

**Acknowledgment is made for quotations from the following:**

"Empowered by Remembering and Hoping," by Walter Brueggemann, in *Evangelism for a New Day,* III, no. 1, May, 1975. Used by permission of the United Church Board for Homeland Ministries (Division of Evangelism, Church Extension and Education).

"Civil Religion and the Bicentennial," by Robert Bellah, in *Bicentennial Broadside,* © 1975. Used by permission of the Working Group on the Bicentennial of the National Council of Churches.

*Extraordinary Living for Ordinary Men,* by Sam Shoemaker. Copyright © 1965 by Zondervan Publishing House. Used by permission.

"From Communism to Christianity," by B. P. Dotsenko, in *Christianity Today,* January 5, 1973. Copyright 1973 by *Christianity Today.* Used by permission.

"A Nativity Narrative," by F. Mallet-Jorris, in *Commonweal,* December 27, 1968. Used by permission of Commonweal Publishing Co., Inc.

Byron Knight and Herman Ahrens' article reprinted with permission from *Youth Magazine,* "Billy Graham: A Personal Conversation," p. 75, March, 1975. Copyright © 1975, United Church Press.

*The Militant Ministry,* by Hans-Ruedi Weber. Copyright © 1967 by Fortress Press. Used by permission.

"The Third Stage of Religion," by David Stoner, April, 1974, and interview with Senator Mark Hatfield, August, 1971, in *Faith at Work.* Reprinted by permission from *Faith at Work* magazine.

From *The Seven Storey Mountain* by Thomas Merton, copyright, 1948, by Harcourt Brace Jovanovich, Inc., and reprinted with their permission. Poem line form used by permission of Argus Communications, as used in *He Is the Still Point of the Turning World* by Mark Link, © 1971.

"Rediscovery of Faith," by Edith Black, in *Radical Religion,* vol. I, no. 1, pp. 18–20. Used by permission.

"Church Education for Tomorrow," by John Westerhoff III. Copyright 1975 Christian Century Foundation. Reprinted by permission from the December 31, 1975 issue of *The Christian Century.*

*Faith Is a Star,* by Roland Gammon. (Mr. Gammon, religious author and lecturer, is the author of *Truth Is One, A God for Modern Man,* and *All Believers Are Brothers.* Address % World Authors Ltd., 655 Madison Ave., N.Y.)

**Library of Congress Cataloging in Publication Data**

Hendrick, John R        1927–
    Opening the door of faith.

    Includes bibliographical references.
    1. Evangelistic work.  2. Faith.  I. Title.
BV3790.H388        269′.2        76-12404
ISBN 0-8042-0675-9

Copyright © 1977 John Knox Press          CTS Press
Copyright © 1983 John R. Hendrick          701 Columbia Drive
Printed in the United States of America     Decatur, Georgia 30030

# Acknowledgments

In a very real sense this is not "my" book. Without wanting to shift responsibility for its viewpoints to others, I do wish to acknowledge some of those without whom it would not have come into print.

Over the years the main shapers of my thought have been Dr. James I. McCord of Princeton Seminary, Dr. C. Ellis Nelson late of Union Seminary, New York, now Louisville Presbyterian Seminary, and more recently Dr. James W. Fowler of The Divinity School, Harvard University.

All they and others taught me has been invigorated and tested by Christians in Presbyterian congregations in Star City, Mt. Zion and Wilmar, Arkansas; Grace, San Antonio, Texas; Fanwood, New Jersey; Westminster, Beaumont, Texas.

The invitation of President Prescott H. Williams and the Faculty of Austin Presbyterian Theological Seminary to deliver the 1973 Settles Lectures in Missions and Evangelism led to changes in my plans for study of moral development. Instead I developed the main themes of this volume; I now view this intrusion as providential!

Encouragement, correction, and not a little prodding, were contributed by editors Ms. Dixie Lee Baker and Joe Baggett, consultant William A. Bryant, Jr., and typist Mrs. Robert A. "Pat" Richardson. They have been not only colleagues but friends.

My parents, my wife's mother, my five children, and most of all my wife, Dorothy Layne Hendrick, supplied the affectional nutrients that motivated and the logistical support which sustained this three-years undertaking.

Whether all you folks like it or not, this is "our" book!

John R. "Pete" Hendrick
The Cedars

Rockport, Texas

# *Contents*

>The book's main emphases are noted; the author's main assumptions are stated.

## THE DOOR OF FAITH

>All over the world people are coming to Christian faith. How faith began in the lives of seven persons is told in their own words. From these accounts two conclusions for evangelism are drawn: People come to faith in diverse ways. No one approach to faith awakening is sufficient; many ways are necessary.

>Secular faiths, other religious faiths, as well as faith in faith are shown to be less than adequate from the Christian perspective. Christian evangelism is carried out in a market place of competing faith claims, where there are no non-believers—only other-believers. Without apology or presumption the church is to call persons to faith centered in Jesus Christ.

>Faith is a relation to Christ with not one but two foci—trust and loyalty. These twin aspects of faith are illustrated in Scripture, church history, and contemporary life. Authentic evangelism will call for faith as trust in Jesus the Savior and faith as loyalty in Jesus the Lord. To emphasize one of these over the other is to present a truncated half-faith.

>Evangelism that is scriptural will present faith in Christ in a manner that encourages free choice from among alternatives. Too often evangelism topples over into indoctrination. When Christ is presented, persons

need to be assisted in a process of careful deliberation looking toward their making a free personal decision. The all-essential work of God's Holy Spirit in an act of faith in this process is explained.

Some evangelistic approaches fit better at one period of life than another. Faith readiness in infancy, early childhood, childhood, adolescence, and adulthood is explored. The purpose is to help evangelists and educators discover appropriate ways of awakening and nurturing the faith of persons at various ages. Full faith as a centered, relational, and personal act is possible only in adolescence or beyond.

## OPENING THE DOOR OF FAITH

After distinguishing between faith, belief, and religion, reasons for establishing a faith priority are given. The argument is not that faith is better than belief or religion—only that it is prior to them. In order not to give aid and comfort to those desiring to return to a false spirituality of the church, the relation of faith priority to social concern is clarified.

Congregations are the most powerful instruments available to the church for evangelism and nurture. Within each there is an interlocking system of faith, belief, and religion. Deficiency at the faith level is the factor most responsible for our present failure in communication of the gospel. Practical steps for overcoming this deficit are suggested.

For most people the "medium" of congregational life is the "message." The Book of Acts presents evangelism as an inseparable triad of word, deed, and community life. Illustrations of these aspects of witness are given. If any one is not incorporated into the life of a congregation, its witness is incomplete. Effective evangelism includes all three.

# OPENING THE DOOR of FAITH

# Introduction

If you like to read travel books before leaving on a journey, these introductory words may satisfy your need for early orientation. Others may wish to start the journey right away with chapter 1, later returning to these pages to gain additional insights into the book's main emphases and the author's assumptions.

In the broad view, there are two major parts to the book. Chapters 1 through 5 portray the New Testament concept of faith as it expresses itself in the life of believers. Here, as much as possible, it is opened to full view. Faith in Christ as a freely chosen relationship of trust and loyalty is shown to be the goal of evangelism and the root from which repentance and conversion emerge. Then in chapters 6 through 8 the congregation as an instrument of God for bringing persons to faith is affirmed and examined. Stress is placed on evangelism's threefold witness—word, deed, and life together.

All that is written is based on two assumptions and two hopes of the author:

*Assumption #1*—That Christian faith is an extremely precious and radical gift of God.

*Assumption #2*—That Christian communities are the most powerful instruments available for transmitting this faith.

*Hope #1*—That the rising generation and estranged-from-God adults—both in and out of the Church—will come to faith in God through Jesus Christ.

*Hope #2*—That parents and pastors, educators and evangelists, leaders of church boards and church members will commit themselves afresh to opening the door of Christian faith.

The chapters are arranged as an explanation of these points-of-view.

It will assist, perhaps reassure, the reader to be aware of the main emphases as well as matters dealt with briefly or not at all.

- While discussing the pediatrics of faith—how it is nurtured    the book's primary concern is with the obstetrics of faith—how it is born and what we can do to assist its emergence.
- While fully convinced that faith arises as a gracious work of God's Holy Spirit and that faith is an answering response to God's act in Christ, the book treats faith mainly from the point-of-view of the people who respond and the activity of the community of faith.
- While a theology of mission, a view of Scripture, and an understanding of the gospel are implied in these pages, they are not explicitly argued—instead, the reader is left with the freedom to supply these essentials from his or her own denominational, confessional, or personal orientation.
- While acknowledging that some individuals in the Christian community have a special gift for sharing faith (Ephesians 4:11), the emphasis here is on the way in which the total life of the community—worship, service, care, social action, nurture, fellowship, etc.—makes the gospel audible, visible, and appealing.
- While aware of the relationship of faith to love and good works such as social service and action, attention is directed to faith itself rather than the various consequences which flow from it.
- While ways and means of sharing faith receive some attention, the primary intent of these pages is to rehabilitate the convictional base upon which methods and programs may be built.

*The purpose of the book is to liberate and energize congregations for an evangelism understood in the following ways:*

1. Evangelism is a work of the Triune God—not *the only* work of God, but *a* work of God.

2. Evangelism aims at bringing persons to faith in Christ—not *anything* or *everything* but *one thing* is its goal—*faith in Christ:* not just *our kind of people* but *all people* are its concern.

3. Evangelism is a task in which God invites his people to be his co-workers—not a work which God does by himself, but *with* and *through his church*.

4. Evangelism is an undertaking of the church which is carried out in not *one* but a great *variety* of ways and means.

If our evangelism is to be in accord with the God who calls us, we need carefully worked out guidelines (criteria) for developing, carrying out, and evaluating programs aimed at bringing persons to faith in Christ. We shall proceed now toward our goal by seeking answers to three questions: What is faith? (chapters 1–4). When are persons ready for faith? (chapter 5). What role does the congregation play in the transmission of faith? (chapters 6–8).

# 1 | *Excavating Faith Origins*

All over the world the door of Christian faith is being opened in people's lives. New faith is emerging in France, Taiwan, the U.S., Brazil, Indonesia, Zaire, and the U.S.S.R. People of every race, language, and nation are experiencing the present work of Christ in their lives.

Christian faith involves one's whole being. Its influences are deep, rich, and personal. The way one sees, feels, and acts toward oneself, others, and the universe is shaped by it. (Philippians 3:4–16; 2 Corinthians 5:16–17)

If we want to know how faith begins, information from real people can be of help. Below in their own words seven women and men tell how they came to faith. (Before reading on you might want to look at item 1 at the end of this chapter under "For Further Reflection"; it offers some suggestions for analyzing these cases.)

**Personal Cases**

## DAVE STONER[1]

In *The Becomers,* Keith Miller quotes Alfred North Whitehead as saying, "Religion runs through three stages if it evolves to its final satisfaction. It is the transition from God the void to God the enemy to God the companion."

I cannot recall a time in my life that I did not believe in God. It never occurred to me to doubt that He existed. Nor did it ever occur to me to doubt that He was my enemy! I knew God was up there somewhere, watching my every move and placing check marks by my name every time I failed to measure up.

In my late teens it occurred to me that if indeed God did take names and keep a list, I was way past due for my personal bolt of lightning . . . but it hadn't happened, and my fear was gone!

God became a void. I had nothing to replace the fear. Still, I acknowledged the reality of God, but much in the same manner that I would acknowledge last year's rain. So what? Knowing He existed had no meaning for me.

I began to seek other "gods" to fill the void that was left when the fear went away: peer group acceptance, alchohol, sex, financial gain, material things, civic involvement—constantly setting a new goal, knowing that when it was attained, I'd feel good about myself and my life would have meaning. However, as soon as the goal was met, the void would still be there, in the deepest part of my being, and I would have to find a new windmill to joust with in order to prove my worth. Nothing ever worked, and the void grew; the loneliness enveloped me. I was alone, afraid, empty.

Then, through God's grace, I chanced to hear two laymen speak in a small Methodist church on a bright March Sunday morning. They spoke of a personal relationship with Jesus Christ. Not once did they mention being good. Not once did they deny the presence of problems in their lives. They shared, simply and clearly, of new value systems, of new lifestyles, of changed relationships with the significant others in their lives. I knew that they had found what I had been striving for so long. But I still didn't know what it was they had found.

As the service closed, I heard words that were to change my life. A third person stood up and said, "Before we sing the closing hymn I just want to tell you that God loves you and I love you." If I had been struck by his open palm, my pain could not have been greater, for I thought, "No, he doesn't love me and nobody else does either." In my pain at last I knew what I had been longing for and seeking for so long. Companionship! A place to belong!

Three days later, doubting that God loved me, but hoping that He did, I went to see one of the speakers. I asked him to tell me more of this man called Jesus. After three hours of arduous struggles, I knelt in the man's office and in my stumbling, awkward way said simply, "Lord, if you'll take the mess in my life, I'll give You a try." He took the mess and we entered into a life-changing relationship. I was no longer alone. The emptiness was gone. The void had been filled!

That was over six years ago. Our relationship continues to grow. I am at last in companionship with God.

## THOMAS MERTON[2]

Thomas Merton tells how he discovered Christ. It happened one summer while he was traveling around Europe on his own.

I don't know how it began—
I found myself looking into churches . . .
The effect of the discovery was tremendous . . .
what a thing it was to come upon . . .
an art that was . . .
urgent in all that it had to say . . .
I began to haunt the churches . . .
And now for the first time in my life
I began to find out something
of who this Person was
that men called Christ . . .
The saints of those forgotten days
had left upon the walls of their churches
a word
which . . . I was able
in some measure to apprehend . . .
But above all,
the most real and most immediate source
[of my knowledge . . . ]
was Christ himself,
present in those churches . . .
And it was he
who was teaching me
who he was,
more directly
than I was capable of realizing . . .
And I bought . . .
the New Testament . . .

And I read more and more
of the Gospels . . .
and my love for the old churches
and their mosaics
grew from day to day.
Soon I was no longer visiting them
for art . . .
something else attracted me:
a kind of interior peace. . . .

EDITH BLACK[3]

When I was at Union Theological Seminary, I encountered God in the liberation movements of which I was a participant—in the civil rights, anti-war, and student movements, and in women's liberation.

My deep involvement in the movement enriched me tremendously and in no way do I look back on it with regret. But *like so many other dedicated radicals I quickly burned out.* Why? For a long time I didn't understand why, but now I think I know. I initially dropped out because my health broke down, but it wasn't this that kept me out, for had I known a loving, empathetic response to being sick on the part of my movement friends I would have regained strength to come back fighting. But that is exactly what I did not experience.

It was in my darkest hour, in the moment of deepest despair, that faith began to well up in me like a bubbling spring. In the midst of my greatest awareness of the tragedy of the human condition, the inevitability of human sin, I began, miraculously, to hope. For through years of suffering I was finally learning to put my trust in God alone.

I saw clearly for the first time that the gospel message is the final solution to the human dilemma, the only answer to the agonizing questions: why is truth so often on the scaffold and wrong so often on the throne? In Christ I saw embodied the suffering love which does not succeed on wordly terms (cross) but is nonetheless victorious (resurrection): the paradox beyond human understanding.

Then I learned to pray, learned from a group of radical

counter-cultural evangelical Christians (CWLF—Christian World
Liberation Front) to whom I turned with a sense of compelling
urgency that I can only see as directed by God. The prayer I
uttered was the first in my life in which I turned to God in true
repentance and acknowledged his (non-sexist) sovereignty over
my life, and, in effect, surrendered. What I experienced in the
*"hour I first believed"* can only be described as *"amazing grace,"*
as a *mighty onrush of love,* as God's unconditional acceptance.

Then began the slow anguishing death of the old self, the long
inner struggle that will never in this lifetime be over. Coming to
know Christ can be likened to culture shock, when all the old
ego-props are knocked down and the rug pulled out from under
one's feet. A maturing relationship with God involves the pain of
continual self-confrontation as well as the joy of self-fulfillment,
continual dying and rising again, continual rebirth, the dialectic of
judgment and grace. For the first time in my life I have begun to
have the strength to face myself as I am, without excuse—but
equally important, without guilt. I know that I am sinful but I
could not bear this knowledge if I did not also know that I am
accepted.

I know now that the struggle to humanize the world, the
revolution, is a continual process without final resolution until
that day when God acts decisively to pull it all together. But as a
Christian I can participate in that struggle without succumbing
either to despair or to false optimism. I can have realism without
cynicism and hope without illusion.

I know I will always be one of Jesus' zealot disciples. . . . I will
always walk the delicate tightrope between an idolatrous tendency to absolutize revolution and a pietistic copout. But it is on that
kind of razor's edge that a Christian must always stand, living in
the tension of being "in the world but not of it."

## BILLY GRAHAM[4]

During my last high school years, my keenest ambition was to
be a professional baseball player.

When I was sixteen, after finishing a game, I was invited to
church. I was told that a "fighting preacher" was to preach. I was

interested, for anything about a scrap or a fight was all I wanted. I
forsook my studies and went to church. To my amazement, it was
a great evangelistic campaign and five thousand people were
gathered.

I sat in the rear of the building, curiously watching all the
strange happenings. I wasn't quite sure what would take place
next. I had always thought of religion as more or less "sissy
stuff," and that a fellow who was going to be an athlete would
have no time for such things. It was all right for old men and girls,
but not for real "he-men" with red blood in their veins.

A great giant of a man stood and began to preach in such a way
as I had never heard a man preach. Halfway through his message
he pointed right in my direction and said, "Young man, you are a
sinner." I thought he was talking to me, so I ducked behind the
person in front of me and hid my face! The idea of his calling me a
sinner!

"Why, I'm as good as anybody," I told myself. "I live a good,
clean, healthy, moral life. I'm even a member of a church, though
I seldom go."

But then he began to quote Scripture. "All have sinned, and
come short of the glory of God." "There is none righteous, no,
not one." For the first time in my life I realized I was a sinner, that
my soul was bound for hell, and that I needed a Saviour. But
when he gave the invitation, I rushed out into the night and made
my way home.

I'll never forget the struggle that followed. All night long I
wrestled and fought. The next day I could hardly wait for
evening, so I could get back to the service. This night I sat near
the front. When the preacher stood this time, he seemed to smile
at me. He said in tenderest tones that "God commendeth his love
toward us, in that, while we were yet sinners, Christ died for us."

When the invitation was given, I made my way to the front with
the others. I gave my hand to the preacher and my heart to the
Saviour. Immediately joy, peace, and reassurance flooded my
soul. My sins, which were many, I knew were gone. For the first
time I had met the Person who became the Hero of my life, Jesus
Christ.

## FRANCOISE MALLET-JORRIS[5]

As a child, I do not believe I ever heard the name of Christ pronounced in our home, or heard any member of the family evoke the possibility of a religiously oriented life—except to criticize it. The only religious person among my relations was my maternal grandmother, a very old, very mild and very quiet lady, of whom it was said with a sort of indulgent pity: she goes to church a lot, or, she is very pious. But her behavior was neither discussed, nor criticized; it seemed to be simply understood; at her age such is quite natural. This is what made religious practice appear to me like a custom of old people, or of certain families, a distinguishing mark without great interest, characterized, in the aged, by keeping a pile of little medals in a purse (my grandmother had many of them, not counting a tiny statue of St. Anthony in a case to which she appealed when she lost something). In the case of children, the sign was evidently the First Communion, received in a white dress with 'a veil. This ceremony made me a little jealous, but not too much. I recall a small classmate asked me if I was not making my First Communion; I answered her, like the reasonable child I was, that as for me, I had had a winter vacation. For I considered these were pleasures of the same order and that you could not have everything.

The only figure of Christ that I knew in childhood was the Infant Jesus who appeared at Christmas. Still, there was no crib in our home, only a Christmas tree. The little Jesus was a child born on that day. Why we celebrated his birth I never quite knew; no doubt because he had been particularly well behaved. This absence of the figure of Christ, even the historic Christ, lasted nearly 20 years for me. If I came across his name in a text or read a Catholic author, a sort of amicable fog would seize my mind, keeping it in the same freedom from curiosity. Christ—that was for other people, a life style which was not mine; or even less, a literary theme, a figure you encounter in a school book, and are not quite sure if he really existed.

Important events, I believe, happen in their own time, and often with an extreme simplicity, apparently by chance. For a long time I owned a Bible. I must have been 12 when a classmate had given it to me. I had found the gift a little eccentric, unusable. I had kept it, I thought, in memory of a friendship which was nonetheless long forgotten. Although I read many books, I had not read that one. It gave me the impression of a school book, and one not on the reading list. Suddenly, at 22 I opened it. I had taken 10 years to perform this act. And once begun (though I would cast it aside and take it up more than once), the book would not allow itself to be again forgotten. For me Christ was made living. . . .

Conversion begins like that for many, it seems to me; it is an encounter with a man before it is an encounter with God. It is a word which, first convincing us and touching us, we yet dare only to half-believe. It is a language, at once the simplest and the most universal, whose secret we attempt to plumb. Can it be that with a vocabulary so humble, similes so ordinary, these parables introduce us imperceptibly into another dimension, into a more real world? Through the humanity of the Christ whom we have encountered and heard like any one of us, his divinity begins progressively to appear. Through language, realities which transcend language progressively begin to be manifested. Through fraternity itself, communion emerges.

In reading the Gospel, which I had the privilege (because I believe that it is a privilege) to discover with a fresh eye, what struck me next was the recognition that I was suddenly the recipient of an extreme liberty. I could have thought, perhaps I had thought, that this new faith was going to reduce me, limit me. How many times did I not hear unbelievers ask me: But, all the same, do you feel free to write what you want? And I have a great deal of trouble explaining to them the extraordinary revelation of Christian liberty in Christ.

## AGNES CAMPBELL[6]

I was born into a Christian home and raised in the Presbyterian faith. Sunday school and church were a regular part of my life from infancy through high school. . . . Church attendance along with accepting Jesus Christ as my personal savior, knowing right from wrong and trying to live by the Ten Commandments made me a Christian as far as I was concerned. It was not until much later in my life that I learned what being a "Christian" really meant.

I was married right out of high school to a man [Roy] who was not a Christian. It was not that he didn't believe in God, he had just never been exposed to the church as I had. He was basically a good person and was more than willing to be married by a minister, join the church and have our child baptized, but that's about where it stopped. Personal commitment or financial commitment was not part of the picture. I didn't argue and before I knew it the church had little meaning for either of us. God was always there if you needed him in an emergency. We existed in this relationship for the first nine years of our marriage.

What we didn't realize was that God had been preparing our hearts for a long time and when some very good friends became Christians, He used them as a means for working in our lives. My husband's relationship with Thom (the friend) was very close and through Thom's witness my husband committed his life to Jesus Christ. . . .

It got to the point that I resented the time he spent with Roy sharing and studying. I wanted a relationship with Christ as much as he did but didn't quite know how to attain it. Fortunately, he sensed my feelings and began including me as much as possible. Suddenly the feeling of being included left me and I began to feel pressured. I began to feel I would never become a Christian because I had not been struck by a flash of light, had a miracle worked in my life or any one of a dozen other experiences other people had had. It was not until my husband and I attended a couple's conference at a local church that I began to understand that all Christians are not on the same level in their Christian growth; that God uses all His people as witnesses regardless of the level of their Christian faith. My husband and I began to have a prayer life together as well as a study life. . . . I feel prayer has been one of the most important factors in the awakening of faith. I had never realized the power of prayer before. During the next few months of our lives we had many direct answers to our prayers. . . . *My whole outlook on living has changed.* Just knowing that I'll never have to face anything (good or bad) alone makes every day worth being alive. *My marriage has been strengthened as has our whole family unit.*

As I see people who are close to me struggling with their lives, I pray that one day they too will open their hearts and receive God's promise of salvation.

## B. P. DOTSENKO[7]

In 1944 my family was "reevacuated" to Ukraine. . . . I was allowed to take a two-month break from my studies at the electrotechnical school to see my parents. On my way to the village where they were staying I contracted pneumonia. It took me about three weeks to recover. One hot and humid afternoon in August I wandered into an old barn in our yard and went to sleep on the haystack. Upon awakening I discovered I had slipped between the hay and the rough wooden back wall of the barn. Struggling to get out I only sank deeper until my bare feet were on the floor below. There at my feet were some copies of an old pre-revolutionary magazine called *Niva* ("The Wheatfield"). I began reading. The life described in *Niva* was quite different from what was told us by Soviet propaganda of the times prior to the October Revolution. I looked further through the bundles of literature stashed there and found a book without a cover. Its pages, yellowed with time, were covered with strange type— ancient Slavic. On opposite pages appeared a Russian translation of the text. I read: "The Gospel of Our Lord Jesus Christ." It was frightening and intriguing.

I hid the book under my shirt and sneaked back to my room. There I resumed reading. It was strange reading. I felt uncomfortable, nearly ridiculous. I had been rather thoroughly brainwashed from this sort of thing into Communist ideology, and I believed in the truthfulness and realism of Communism.

. . . But it sank deep, nevertheless.

In 1945 I quit the electrotechnical school and went to a university in Lvov to study at the faculty of physics and mathematics there. One of the most fundamental laws of nature that interested me was the law of entropy, concerning the most probable behavior of the particles (molecules, atoms, electrons, etc.) of any system. If given to itself it will decay very quickly, inasmuch as particles composing any system have a tendency to run wild. It means that all the material world should have turned into a cloud of chaotic dust a long, long time ago. I thought about this, and it dawned upon me that the world is being held in existence by a non-material power that is capable of overruling this destructive entropy. I began to realize, moreover, that the most brilliant scientists in the best equipped laboratories still are incapable of copying even the simplest cell. I started to pray and worship God. It was in the early fifties.

In 1954 I obtained my Ph.D. in physical and mathematical sciences and was assigned to work in the Academy of Sciences of the U.S.S.R. on intercontinental and space rocket research. During this period my personal ideology was swinging further away from Communism.

I was regarded as a successful scientist and was appointed head of the nuclear laboratory of the Kiev State University. In October, 1966, I was called to Moscow, to the Central Committee of the Soviet Communist party. I was told that I would be sent to Canada and after that to Vienna to the International Atomic Energy Agency. There, working as a senior member of the scientific staff, I was supposed to supply the Soviet espionage system with the most important information about the achievements in nuclear research throughout the world. Comrade Baskakov, one of the top men in the party, received me. Lifting up his finger to indicate a quotation from the highest source he said, "We can reward your service very greatly, up to the Nobel Prize." Two days later I was in Canada, at the University of Alberta. When I started to unpack my luggage in the room given to me I pulled out a drawer. There was a book, the Holy Bible, placed by the Gideons. My hands trembled when I took it. I applied for political asylum. The Soviets were furious. Although they failed to make the Canadian government expel me, they managed through their sympathizers to create such an atmosphere at the university that I felt it better to leave. I could not get a job at any other university, so I went to teach in a high school at Yellowknife in the Northwest Territories. Before going there I asked a minister in Edmonton to baptize me. I became a Christian.

**How Faith Begins**

What can be learned about how faith begins from only seven brief "personal testimonies"? Some things certainly—but your own story, that of your friends and other Christians around the world, living and dead, would be required to get a complete understanding of the way people come to Christian faith. Nonetheless, there are some hints that you might want to discuss with others.

1. Each of the seven persons had an experience of The Transcendent One that might be termed mystical or spiritual; each identified this One as Jesus Christ or the God spoken of in the Bible.

2. Several of the persons had what we would call a Christian upbringing. Thus their new faith was like an awakening from a long sleep. Others had no previous Christian ties of any significance; their new faith was a "creation out of nothing"—a surprising new birth.

3. The influence of members of the Christian community seems to have been present in each case. Several were influenced by living Christians; others, however, were influenced by those long dead, e.g. the writers of the New Testament gospels and artisans of medieval cathedrals.

4. A number of these cases would tend to support the generally held view that adolescence and young adulthood are the times in the life cycle when persons have greatest readiness for a faith commitment. (See chapter 5.)

5. The terms "repentance," "conversion," "new birth," "new creation" have applicability to these stories as well as the word "faith." As defined in Chapters 2, 3, and 4, faith is a large concept encompassing the realities denoted by these terms.

Besides these thoughts, here are two conclusions which merit special emphasis:

THERE IS NO ONE WAY PEOPLE COME TO FAITH IN CHRIST. Edith, David, B. P., Thomas, Billy, Francoise, Agnes—each came to Christ in a different manner. C. S. Lewis believed in God first, then in Jesus Christ. A 55-year-old man told me recently that he became a follower of the human Jesus and only much later came to believe in God the Father. Some come to Christ through reading a novel or by studying a Gospel. Some believe because of the influence of a Christian group. Others find faith through the testimony of a single individual. Some begin their Christian life deeply convicted of sin and seek Christ's forgiveness. Others start, not so much from a sense of personal sin or need, but because they see the cause of God and offer their strength to it. For some the coming of faith is like the dawn; for others its advent is like a flash of lightning. Such is the variety discovered when one examines the ways persons come to faith.

If we could sort and catalogue all factors in the faith genesis of all Christians, we would, I believe, be awed by the diversity of ways in which the one reality, Jesus Christ, is received. The light of Christ is refracted into an infinite variety of hues in the life of each individual.

THERE IS NO ONE WAY TO BRING PEOPLE TO FAITH IN CHRIST. A revival preacher in the rural South, cathedral art of medieval Europe, a long ignored gift Bible, a friend's influence on a husband, a weathered Russian translation of the Gospels, a layman's witness in a little church—these and a thousand other means and methods God uses to bring people to faith in Himself. This seems to be a self-evident truth. Unless we pause to think about it, we sometimes feel that one particular way is the best way—usually the way our faith began, or the way most people in our denomination came to faith.

It often seems that congregations and denominations develop a limited number of standardized approaches to opening the door of faith. Many of our churches offer the communicant or confirmation route as the highway to God—busloads of children are driven down it every Lenten season. Four decades ago H. Richard Niebuhr caricatured another tendency to uniformity: "Regeneration, the dying of the self and the rising to new life . . . becomes conversion which takes place on Sunday morning during the singing of the last hymn or twice a year when the revival preacher comes to town." (*The Kingdom of God in America,* p. 179.)

In more recent times we have added other approaches. We have developed sales-oriented visitation schemes with questions to ask, right answers to give, and appeals to make. The latest "new and better" ways to open the door of faith are relational evangelism with its use of small groups, lay renewal gatherings, and a "counseling" approach to personal witnessing. These represent the ingenuity of Christians who care enough to share their faith with others. But—and this is the point—*no one way is the way.* This is not an attack on means and methods in evangelism. They are essential; in fact, each is a way. Yet, if our approaches are too few or too standardized, we can often be guilty of making the spirits of children and adults fit our precut patterns. God's ways are too unlimited for such methodological narrowness.

In his dealings with us God takes into account the splendid uniqueness of each of us. Any nurture or evangelism worthy of his name will seek to do the same.

Having seen how faith in Christ mixes with the reason, experience, emotion and relationship of living persons, we now turn to examine the phenomena of faith itself (chapters 2, 3, 4).

**FOR FURTHER REFLECTION**

1. As you work through these faith accounts, you might want to use these or other questions to assist in digging out significant data:
    a. Where did the person's faith begin—in what social and geographical situation?
    b. What was the person's religious or church relationship, if any, prior to the emergence of faith?'
    c. When did the person's faith begin—over what span of years, or at what age?
    d. By whom, or by what, was the person's new faith called forth or awakened?
    e. Upon whom or what was the person's faith centered?
    f. Was there evidence of faith as a relationship of trust; a relationship of loyalty?
    g. Was their faith decision freely made, or was there indoctrination or coercion?
    h. What indicators of change in feeling, attitude, or behavior resulted from the person's new found faith?
    i. What do we learn about God's way of working from these accounts?

2. If you want to record what you learn from this study, you can divide an 8½ × 11 sheet of paper as follows, recording your answer in the appropriate square.

| Questions | Dave Stoner | Thomas Merton | etc. | | |
|---|---|---|---|---|---|
| Where faith began | | | | | |
| Religious affiliation before faith | | | | | |
| etc. | | | | | |
| | | | | | |
| | | | | | |
| | | | | | |
| | | | | | |

After you have filled out the sheet, make a list of conclusions, questions, problems, and issues that you want to think more about or discuss with others. If you are studying with a class, a plan should be made to share findings with each other.

3. You and others in your church have your own stories of how your faith began. These could be shared in a class meeting, with the understanding that anyone who wants to can "pass."

4. The classical biblical account of how faith began is that of the Apostle Paul. (See Acts 9, 22, 26, Philippians 3, etc.) This could be analyzed by using the questions and chart above.

5. In this chapter, what learning did you make which would be good advice for someone who wants to open the door of faith for another person—a parent, church school teacher, a pastor, friend at the office, etc?

6. As this chapter makes plain, people often look back to some peak spiritual experience. Is that a good thing to do? How is it helpful? Could it be harmful? Think about this and discuss it. Here are two quotations that may aid your reflection. The first is by an unidentified author; the second is by the Scottish theologian Donald Baillie.

   Admittedly religious experiences are real for many people and mark the beginning of their pilgrimage of faith. Taken in the proper perspective, there can be genuine religious experience in which faith is clarified, sins are acknowledged, forgiveness is accepted, and salvation is assured. From this initial stage of their life in discipleship, those people proceed to lead dedicated private and public lives witnessing to the presence and power of God. On the other hand, for many, these religious experiences are both the beginning and end of their journey of faith, and they remain in their self-centered, stagnant position as the personally redeemed. At best, they may seek to share their type of private religion and covet the same experiences for others.

   Memories of this kind invigorate us in times of spiritual dryness. But the main thing is to have a living religion here in the present. It is a poor thing to have the experience of God in one's past but not in one's present.

7. In this chapter we have been looking at religious experience. C. S. Lewis says that it is important to turn away from the experience itself and instead to focus on the object of the experience. What does he mean? Why would he urge this? What are the dangers, if any, of emphasizing one over the other? For some further reflection—not an answer—read 2 Corinthians 12:1–10. The next chapter will also be helpful.

8. There seems to be a criticism of "standardized approaches to opening the door of faith" such as revivals, communicant classes, visitation evangelism, etc. What point is being made? Can an organization such as a church deal with every person on an individual basis? Should that really be our goal? How can "standardized approaches" be made responsive to each person's situation?

# 2 | Faith as a Centered Act

A major goal of every Christian and congregation is to open the door of faith. But what exactly is faith? How will it be recognized when it appears? What are its characteristic features?

Answers are complex because faith has many components. Three will receive our attention—faith as a personal act, faith as a relational act, and faith as a centered act. Together these provide an adequate, though by no means total, picture of the phenomena of faith.

In this chapter secular faiths, other religious faiths, and faith in faith are shown to be less than adequate from a Christian perspective. Christian evangelism is carried out in a market place of competing faith claims where there are no non-believers—only other-believers. Without apology, but without presumption, the church is to call persons to faith centered in Jesus Christ.

## Faith in Faith

Before the turn of the century, William James, the renowned psychologist, had experiences which led him to the view that faith is absolutely essential for human well-being:

> One evening there fell upon me without warning a horrible fear of my own existence. There arose in my mind the image of an epileptic patient whom I had seen in the asylum, a black-haired youth with greenish skin, looking absolutely non-human. *That shape am I,* I felt, potentially. Nothing that I possess can defend me against that fate if the hour for it should strike for me as it struck for him. I became a mass of quivering fear. I remember wondering how other people could live, how I

myself had ever lived, so unconscious of that pit of insecurity beneath the surface of life.[1]

This terrible depression in his late twenties nearly drove him to suicide. Eventually he recovered, but only after deciding that he must have "the will to believe" in a higher power. James then began a study of religious experience. He collected stories of religious conversion which, first published in 1902, became a classic. *The Varieties of Religious Experience* argues that deep religious conviction is vital for human life.

Perhaps without realizing it, James was discovering and reinforcing the insights of another nineteenth century genius, Leo Tolstoi, who wrote:

From the beginning of the human race, whenever there is life there is faith which makes life possible. . . . Without faith it is impossible to live.[2]

To assert the human significance of believing is not easy. In their day James and Tolstoi must have felt like voices in a wilderness of empiricism and rationalism. Many still view faith as synonomous with superstition—unworthy of and unneeded by modern man.

Yet today good psychological evidence supports its all important role. Erik Erikson, the psychoanalyst, popularly known for his eight stages of the life cycle, is one who has demonstrated that faith as trust (stage 1) and fidelity (stage 5) are critical components for human growth. (Chapter 5, "Readiness for Faith," explains Erikson's views in detail).

This growing conviction among students of human behavior is put into clear focus by priest-psychologist Eugene Kennedy:

To believe . . . is as essential to man as air and water. . . . Believing is an essential human function without which it is impossible to understand or to integrate one's personality. . . . man hungers to believe in order to have a sense of meaning and purpose.[3]

Calling persons to faith makes a clear contribution to human welfare. We can be grateful for this new clarity on the role of faith in human existence.

Some designate this way of thinking as "faith in faith." Rene

Padilla of the World Congress on Evangelization called it "believism." Catholics refer to this position as "indifferentism." Popularly put, it comes to this:

Have a good strong faith. It will help you live a satisfying and useful life. What you believe isn't important so long as your faith is sincere and strong.

## Religious Faiths

The psychological arguments for this view find impressive support among some students of world religions. For example, it has been argued that in a broader sense that the Apostle Paul (Romans 4) or Christian theology ever anticipated, salvation is by faith, not just faith in Christ, however, but faith derived from the tradition of any living religion. According to Wilfred C. Smith, former Professor of World Religions at Harvard University, each of these traditions through its particular symbol system affords for the believer a reach into the ultimate.[4]

Though these religions differ markedly, each is felt to be adequate in its own way. The impact of this kind of thinking is now widespread, as this selection from a study guide prepared for use in major denominations in the U.S.A. indicates:

As Christians learn accurately about beliefs of others, they will discover that each of the great religions stresses and exemplifies values and virtues of universal significance. It can be humbling to realize that some basic Christian teachings are followed more faithfully by Muslims or Buddhists than by the average church member. Perhaps the answer to the puzzling dilemma facing the Christian—Do I try to force my faith on someone else or do I accept all faiths as equally good?—has just one answer. God has chosen to reveal himself and his will to many people in many different ways. It is impossible to deny the spirit of God in the great religions of the world. To do so would be an attempt to limit the transcendent power of God.

The missionary role in today's world seems to be that of growing in one's own faith as one grows in the appreciation of others.[5]

This is the popular view but from a Christian perspective strange indeed.

It certainly does not square with Scripture, nor can it be justified from the perspective of classic Christian theology.

## Secular Faiths

Besides the great religious traditions of East and West, our planet has a thriving crop of secular faiths—money, *Playboy* sex, technology, racism, humanism, success, nationalism, hedonism, to name a few. Cynthia Wedel's description of two may help us visualize their reality.

1. For an increasing number it is faith in technology. People have discovered and invented many wonderful things in the past century, and are now becoming aware of problems such as pollution, population explosion and environmental hazards brought about by technology. But the faithful believe sincerely that, having come this far, technology can also find solutions to these new problems.

2. Humanism is an increasingly popular faith today. It says that human beings are essentially good, and that the things which are wrong in the world come about because the arrangements of society have gone awry. If people will use their good will and good sense, and are helped to do so, perhaps someday a better and more perfect world will be built. Humanism can be a very lofty and inspiring faith and has developed some great leaders.[6]

We rightly sense that these "isms" exert a godlike power over masses of people. Of a variety of reasons for this, one seems uppermost.

Around each of these "gods" is a community of true believers. These believers have confidence that "good" will come to them and others from these "gods." The cause represented by these "idols" is faithfully served—often by "evangelistically" communicating their worth and benefit. Theologian H. Richard Neibuhr uses the term "social faith" to describe this phenomena. In this he refers to a wide variety of human communities which embody a well defined world view and value system.[7] Family, tribe, race, corporation, denomination, nation, state—are among possible social vehicles of a particular faith. From such social sources persons derive their understanding of right and wrong, their sense of personal worth, their confidence in the future, and to such collectivities they yield their highest fealty. The pressure on individuals from them is vast and pervasive. Every member of the human family is influenced by one or more of these groups. It is this way that the gods of this world become lively faith options for all of us.

**Faith in Christ**

Does the object of one's faith make a difference? Does it matter which religion, secular or traditional, we espouse?

Theologian Paul Tillich gives an affirmative answer. For him, false or misdirected faith leads to "existential disappointment" and potentially to the very destruction of the personality.[8] A long tradition of "gods that failed" literature supports his view. The book of Ecclesiastes, the confessions of Augustine and Tolstoi, the more recent autobiography of C. S. Lewis are only a few examples of persons who reached the conclusion that not just any "god" will do; the object of faith is determinative of the adequacy of faith. For those named above, only faith in God revealed in the Bible proved in the end to be sufficient to their deepest needs and longings.

For the Old and New Testaments, the object of one's faith is of critical significance. So much so that one might conclude from a careful reading that the Bible views sin not so much as misdeeds but as misplaced faith. Be that as it may, the word of Scripture on the faith object question is not in doubt.

"I am the LORD your God, who brought you out of the land of Egypt, out of the house of bondage.
You shall have no other gods before me." (Exodus 20:2-3)

"And there is salvation in no one else, for there is no other name under heaven given among men by which we must be saved." (Acts 4:12)

Jesus said to him, "I am the way, and the truth, and the life; no one comes to the Father, but by me." (John 14:6)

By way of summary, E. C. Blackman in the *Interpreter's Dictionary of the Bible*'s article on "Faith" writes:

In its specifically Christian meaning "faith" is faith in God's decisive activity through Christ for man's [every person's] redemption. . . . It was not a general belief in God. . . . For the New Testament, Christ is the new focus of faith.

It is this biblical orientation which led the Presbyterian Church, U.S. to adopt its statement on evangelism which reads in part: "Evangelism seeks to present Jesus Christ as *the only* Savior and Lord."

Professor Walter Brueggemann of Eden Seminary, United Church of Christ, put the matter this way:

We have been through a time when there has been a failure of nerve. We lacked confidence about our language, our vision of reality and the life-giving role the church could play. But courage to engage in mission and boldness for evangelism never comes from lack of confidence or from failure of nerve. The remarkable shifting moods of faith in the church currently let us articulate our distinctiveness in a world of competing faith claims and alternative loyalties. It is time to face up to our peculiarness.

Being distinctive is not to claim we are better. The claim does not mean our morality is better; nor do we claim that our life is more disciplined, nor that our hope is more fervent. It means rather that we are peculiar not in the marginal matters that are so visible to casual observers, but that we are different at the core of our life. We shall not be free in our mission nor faithful in our evangelism until that distinctiveness at the core is affirmed.[9]

The "distinctiveness at the core" is Jesus Christ.

The church is the only human community which professes this center of fidelity and source of confidence. At the very least, this creates tension between us and every faith rooted in secular society or traditional religion. The Bible is plain. Our faith commitment to Jesus means a loyalty to him surpassing that given to any other person or group (Matthew 6:24). While this does not mean that a Christian may disregard or disparage social or religious loyalties (Romans 13, Ephesians 6), it leaves us no doubt that Jesus Christ must be first in one's life.

**The Christian's Struggle for Faith in a World of Many Faiths**

As we live in the world committed to Jesus Christ, many of us feel surrounded by a welter of less than ultimate faith claims. We who belong to the household of Christian faith also belong to the household of a family, a corporation, a region, a nation, etc. Belonging exacts a high price because we are expected to believe, support, and be loyal to the values and world views of each. This is the modern equivalent of temptation to idolatry of which we read in the Old Testament. Responding Christianly is both complex and challenging. This issue could be discussed in terms of life in a family or business corporation. Instead, because of our focus on American traditions during the late 1970's, we will probe the relation between faith centered in Jesus Christ and faith in the national state.

From Caesar's Rome to Hitler's Germany, down to the present day, nations have asserted themselves as "savior" and "lord." How this functions in modern nationalism has been described in the following way:

When the patriotic nationalist says "I was born to die for my country," he is exhibiting . . . faith. The national life is for him the reality whence his own life derives its worth. He relies on the nation as source of his own value. . . . His life has meaning because it is part of that context, like a word in a sentence. . . . His trust may also be directed toward the nation as a power which will supply his needs, care for his children, and protect his life. . . . He values the center and seeks to enhance its power and glory. He makes that center his cause for which to live and labor. . . . The creedal expressions of patriotism . . . are . . . used to pledge devotion; they are spoken and sung by voices ringing with resolution; they may signalize one's decision to give everything to the country's cause.[10]

This note of religious fervor was in a postcard that came to my desk: "Christians can, and certainly should, celebrate our nation's 200th anniversary—the Church should have a great showing of patriotism. . . . America, we should *work for* and *love above all else!*" The first two sentences we can all affirm; however, the last sentence, if taken at face value, is a lapse into idolatry.

The peril of giving too much devotion to country is clearly (but oppositely) seen by liberals and conservatives in the United States. Liberals warn against the state's pretentious demands for unqualified loyalty; conservatives warn against the state's pretentious offer of absolute cradle-to-grave care. Both serve us well— the one by steering us away from the temptation to give it our highest allegiance; the other by warning against becoming overly dependent on the nation's welfare. There is always a sinister possibility that persons will endow our nation or some other with such divine rights and powers. Christians, whose call is to give loyalty and trust to the Transcendent One as Lord and Savior, have and must continue to resist deifying the nation state. Our call is to respect but not worship our country.

From the origin of our country to the present time, this spirit has been carried forward by what sociologist Robert Bellah has called "the great tradition in civil religion in America."

America was founded by religious men and women—people who were far from perfect or guiltless, but people who recognized their "final dependence" on a God who entirely transcended the nation and to whose judgment they felt it was subject. . . . We thus have a long and unbroken tradition of civil religion in this nation that differs from that of the Roman Empire or the modern nationalisms which express unbroken devotion to the nation as its own end. Idolatrous nationalism and idolatrous civil religion have not been lacking in America, but they have never gone unchallenged. . . . It is not a tradition in which "the success of a particular nation" is the ultimate measure. It is a tradition that calls the nation to repentance when it violates those moral and religious standards that transcend it. . . . Many times before the churches—or, at least a remnant from the churches—have called this nation to account, have called it to return to its own highest religious commitments, have called it to abandon idolatry and renew its faith in truth and justice. Perhaps, on the occasion of the Bicentennial, it will be possible again to call the nation back to a civil religion that is higher than patriotism and both hallows and limits patriotism.[11]

If we are serious about evangelism, we must distinguish the

Christian faith even from the great tradition of American civil religion. What is at stake here is sometimes hard to see. So much in our national history and American value system has been derived from biblical sources that many see no difference between the two. But there is a difference of crucial significance. Rehearse for yourself the American story—Pilgrim fathers, freedom of worship, promised land, Washington, liberty and justice for all, Lincoln, this nation under God, in God we trust, inaugural prayers, etc. Bred out of our national religious ethos for a variety of practical political reasons, but nonetheless left out, is any reference to Jesus Christ the center of God's plan.

Despite this difference there is no need for Christians to disparage the national faith. Rather, we should respect its positive values, as we would those of any other living religion or way of life, yet guard against it as a temptation to idolatry.

There is no one Christian answer as to how to work out the tension between Christ and country. It is a struggle in which we daily are engaged. In a recent interview Mark Hatfield, United States Senator from Oregon, gave some of his own thoughts on the subject:

I would not be so presumptuous as to present myself as an example of "the Christian stance" on this question. As an individual I've found certain ways to handle it and live with myself and my convictions:

First, I have a list of priorities as to where my allegiance and commitment is made. My commitment is first to God and to Jesus Christ, to my family, and to my country. My political party ranks down the list a bit. I have loyalty to it, but to a lesser degree.

When people are confronted with controversial issues and when various viewpoints are expressed to them by groups organized to persuade or influence them one way or another, they still have to consider their own priorities. . . .

Second, I can't take the road of consulting public opinion polls, developing a consensus, and voting the most "popular" position. . . .

When the question came up of continuing the supersonic transport plane project, many of the economic interests in Oregon indicated that it would be to the state's advantage to vote for the SST. I considered all the factors and felt I could not in good conscience vote for it, and in spite of the economic pressures I voted no.

There are always tensions and pressures, but I still feel that if you remain true to your basic priorities of commitment and conviction people will respect you in the long run. They will see that it is an honest position rather than one dictated by political expediency.[12]

Authentic faith in Christ frees us from all false claims. It is *the* declaration of independence which God desires to hear from all people. To be fully in Christ is to discover the liberty of living under a supra-national God with a supra-cultural outlook. Such persons in every country are equipped with the inner freedom to be, at one and the same time, responsible citizens, ready critics, and reasonable reformers.

### Faith in the Market Place

The task of the church is to open the door of Christian faith. Yet this is never done in a vacuum—religious and secular faiths abound. Like merchants in a global market place many faiths are being hawked—sincerely, openly, and determinedly. It is in this "religious" world that the church is called to the work of evangelism.

There are no *non*-believers; there are only *other*-believers. Everyone has some faith. Thus a call to Christian faith is an appeal to turn away from one's god or gods to the One, the true and living God in Christ (1 Thessalonians 1:9). True evangelism asks for a break with one's religious and secular allegiances. Faith in Christ involves a permanent revolution of mind and heart—a reorientation of life—repentance, conversion!

This is not always understood in the church. Because church members are indelibly stamped with the impress of their own social, regional, and class values—pollutants of racism, sexism, militarism, nationalism, and other-worldliness stain our con-sciousness—it is difficult for us to do the work of evangelism with the ultimate seriousness the task demands.

In a diabolical manner some American religious leaders have

discovered that there is a potent mass audience appeal in setting aside radical Christian faith for an adulterous blend of God and country, Christ and humanism, religion and race, Jesus and success, etc. They name the God of the Bible and proceed on his behalf to present arms, glorify humans in the highest, baptize racism, or bless success. The Old Testament is full of stories of persons who professed the Lord God and then proceeded to bow down to the gods of the land. (Cf. the Book of Judges). Then and now the name of such activity is idolatry! Growth on these terms clearly does not contribute to the upbuilding of the body of Christ—though it may enlarge membership rolls and enrich coffers. We cannot be content with such cultural debasement of the gospel. The promise of an authentic evangelism centered in Jesus Christ as only Savior and Lord is that our churches will become his church!

**FOR FURTHER REFLECTION**

1. One way to reflect on the main themes of this chapter is to jot down your reactions to the following quotations from it—or, if you're studying with others, to ask a person or two to prepare some comments on a particular one to share with the group. Any one of these can be debated pro or con:

   "There are no non-believers; there are only *other-* believers. Everyone has some faith."

   "To believe . . . is as essential to persons as air and water."

   "What you believe isn't important so long as your faith is sincere and strong."

   "The Bible views sin not so much as misdeeds as misplaced faith."

   "Without apology or presumption the Church is to call persons away from these (religious and secular faiths) to faith centered in Jesus Christ."

2. Being tolerant of others and respecting their religious freedom is very important. Some people, Christians included, have a feeling that evangelism—sharing faith in Christ with others—borders on intolerance and a lack of respect for others. Pope Paul VI spoke to this issue not long ago. He said the religious freedom of non-Roman Catholics was not violated by evangelization and called for a revival of missionary fervor in the church. In one of his longest declarations, the Pope said that it would certainly be an error to impose something on the con-

sciences of our brethren . . . but evangelization, or the spreading of the gospel to the world, represented not an attack on religious liberty, but an offer of the choice of a way that even nonbelievers consider noble and uplifting. Why should only falsehood and error, debasement and pornography have the right to be put before people and unfortunately imposed on them by the destructive propaganda of the mass media, by the tolerance of legislation, the timidity of the good and the impudence of the wicked?

The respectful presentation of Christ and his kingdom is more than the evangelizer's right; it is his duty. It is likewise the right of his fellow men to receive from him the proclamation of the good news of salvation.[13]

Do you agree that evangelism is not a violation of religious freedom or conscience of others? Is it possible for evangelism to be carried out in such a way that it is an act of intolerance? Why would the Pope need to make such an appeal to Catholics? Is his message a good word for Protestants, too?

3. The church, i.e. people like ourselves, always live in the midst of a particular culture. In some ways we are like the people around us. In some ways we differ. Read this description of early Christians. How were the early Christians like, and how unlike, their neighbors?

Christians are not distinguished from the rest of mankind either in locality or in speech or in customs. For they dwell not somewhere in cities of their own, neither do they use some different language, nor practice an extraordinary kind of life. Nor again do they possess any invention discovered by any intelligence or study of ingenious men, nor are they masters of any human dogma as some are. But while they dwell in cities of Greeks and barbarians as the lot of each is cast, and follow the native customs in dress and food and the other arrangements of life, yet the constitution of their own citizenship, which they set forth, is marvelous, and confessedly contradicts expectation. They dwell in their own countries, but only as sojourners; they bear their share in all things as citizens, and they endure all hardships as strangers. Every foreign country is a fatherland to them, and every fatherland is foreign. They marry like all other men and they beget children; but they do not cast away their offspring. They have their meals in common, but not their wives. They find themselves in the flesh, and yet they live not after the flesh. Their existence is on earth, but their citizenship is in heaven. They obey the established laws, and they surpass the laws in their own lives. They love all men, and they are persecuted by all.

—Epistle to Diognetus

For ourselves how should we be like or unlike our family, our school, our region, our company, our nation? What does being "in but not of this world" have to do with our ability to do the work of evangelism?

4. "As I look around it appears that there are many 'Jesus Christs.' The materialists go to church and ask God to bless their lives and styles of living in the name of Jesus; so do the racists, the militarists, etc. . . . When it comes to evangelism—when we ask a person to consider Jesus—immediately we have the problem of whether in fact we are communicating the living Jesus or some cultural substitute." (Florida Pastor).

In many ways these are confusing words. Is it true that the Church is presenting "many 'Jesus Christs'"? Is this done intentionally? Inadvertently? What might a cultural substitute for the living Jesus be like? Has this pastor fingered one of the big troubles with evangelism in your church or in your denomination?

5. The following was reported by Religious News Service.

Brooks Hays, former Congressman from Arkansas and a past president of the Southern Baptist Convention (SBC), called on Christians to remember that the government must be respected but never worshipped.

Addressing members of the SBC Christian Life Commission at a dinner, . . . Mr. Hays asserted that "honest patriotism requires disagreement with the government when it is wrong as well as praise for it when it is right. True patriotism should involve a compassion for the nation which is consistent and objective."

Mr. Hays warned that "an awesome civil religion now threatens the nation and blurs the distinction between what belongs to Caesar and what belongs to God. This culture faith does not threaten to replace our biblical faith—only to compromise it. Confessors of the folk faith tend to equate God and country. Civil religion is characterized by the mytholgical self-identity of America as a Christian nation and by the superficial loyalty of the patriot who confesses, 'My country right or wrong!'"

During the Bicentennial celebration, the former SBC president predicted, "Temptations to succumb to the appeals of culture religion will abound."

Offering guidelines for observing the Bicentennial, Mr. Hays advised, "We must carefully distinguish between our loyalty to the nation and our faithfulness to God. Though the nation is important, it is not ultimate. Though politics are of tremendous significance, their significance is not absolute. The maintenance of such a distinction will keep us from using religious motives to gain support for civil policies and likewise from using the institutions of government to do the work of religion."

Do you find these comments helpful, troubling, confusing, mistaken? Write out and share with others your own views on the subject of God and Caesar.

# 3 | *Faith as a Relational Act*

Being a Christian is not primarily a matter of right thinking, right feeling, or right behaving. Most of all it is a right relationship—a relationship of faith in God through Jesus Christ which then deeply interpenetrates one's thoughts, emotions and behavior.

Faith as a relational act is a response with not one but two foci—trust and loyalty. Webster's Third International Dictionary defines faith as "The act or state . . . of having confidence in God and of being loyal to his will. . . . " An examination of the article on "faith" in *A Theological Dictionary of the New Testament* shows that the dominant, though not the exclusive, meaning of faith resides in these twin concepts of trust and loyalty.[1]

### Faith as Trust

In faith as trust we relate to God as sin forgiving, worth bestowing, life sustaining, death defeating. Our stance before him is primarily one of dependence, receptivity, passivity. In this orientation we approach God—primarily as Savior with our needs for safety, love, acceptance, esteem. A typical prayer of faith as trust is, "Our Father . . . Give us this day our daily bread . . . Forgive us our debts. . . ."

Rose Kennedy provides a moving statement of a trustful relationship to God.

I have come to the conclusion that the most important element in human life is faith.

If God were to take away all His blessings, health, physical fitness, wealth, intelligence, and leave me but one gift, I would ask for faith—for with faith in Him, in His goodness, mercy, love for me, and belief in everlasting life, I believe I could suffer the loss of my other gifts and still be happy—trustful, leaving all to His inscrutable providence. When I start my day with a prayer of consecration to Him, with complete trust and confidence, I am perfectly relaxed and happy regardless of what accident of fate befalls me because I know it is part of His divine plan and He will take care of me and my dear ones.[2]

**Faith as Loyalty**

In faith as loyalty we relate to God as nature controlling, history directing, nation ruling, person calling. Our position before him is primarily one of servant, co-worker, partner, agent. In this orientation we approach God primarily as Lord with our need for building, contributing, cooperating, and actualizing his and our purposes. A typical prayer of faith as loyalty is "Our Father . . . Thy Kingdom come, Thy will be done. . . ."

Congressman John Anderson, Republican from Illinois and a devout conservative Christian, had an experience which illumines faith as a relationship of loyalty. Anderson and the majority of his constituents opposed the open housing legislation before Congress in 1968. Yet—after "prayer, meditation and careful consideration of my responsibility as a Christian" he voted for passage of the bill. Obviously to him being loyal to the will of God as he understood it was a significant aspect of his faith relation to the Father; it was so strong, in fact, that it enabled him to transcend other claimant loyalties—to himself and those who elected him.

For Jesus faith in God evidenced these two responses. In discussing the prayers of Jesus, J. Jeremias describes his relation to God in a way that clearly reflects trust and confidence: "Jesus spoke to God like a child to its father, simply, inwardly, confidently."[3]

That faith for Jesus also contained the element of loyalty or fidelity is clear from even the simplest reading of his life story. At the beginning we find him saying, "I must be about my Father's business"; toward the end he is praying, "Not my will but thine be done"; and, finally, he gives his life to finish the work that God has given him to do.

Besides Jesus, other biblical figures like Abraham and Moses provide prototypical examples of this dual nature of faith as the Book of Hebrews makes plain.

By faith Abraham obeyed when he was called to go out to a place which he was to receive as an inheritance; and he went out, not knowing where he was to go. By faith he sojourned in the land of promise, as in a foreign land, living in tents with Isaac and Jacob, heirs with him of the same promise. For he looked forward to the city which has foundations, whose builder and maker is God. (Hebrews 11:8–10)

By faith Moses, when he was grown up, refused to be called the son of Pharaoh's daughter, choosing rather to share ill-treatment with the people of God than to enjoy the fleeting pleasures of sin. He considered abuse suffered for the Christ greater wealth than the treasures of Egypt, for he looked to the reward. By faith he left Egypt, not being afraid of the anger of the king; for he endured as seeing him who is invisible. By faith he kept the Passover and sprinkled the blood, so that the Destroyer of the first-born might not touch them. (Hebrews 11:24–28)

To trust God and to obey Him—that is what it means to have faith in the full biblical sense.

With H. Richard Niebuhr we can see how such an understanding of faith enlarges our understanding of "I believe" in The Apostles' Creed:

The Christian statement, "I believe in God, the Father, Almighty Maker of heaven and earth," is on the one hand an expression of confidence, on the other, an oath of allegiance. In one sense it means, "I trust in God;" in the other, "I will keep faith with him."[4]

From the earliest centuries new Christians have been called to such a profession. Hans-Ruedi Weber's reconstructed baptismal account further clarifies this double aspect of faith as integral to the life of the believer.

The place is the island of Rhodes; the time is the fifth century A.D.

. . . On an Easter morning . . . Even before cockcrow a group of people, for the most part probably slaves, gathered at a place for baptism. . . . This handful of people of Rhodes had come to know Christ. The message of an evangelist or more likely the strange quality of life of the Christians who lived among them had caught their attention. . . . Now they had gathered at that baptistry which reminded them of the cross of Christ. Each one turned to the dark west and cried into this darkness: "I renounce you, Satan, and all your service and all your works!" . . . Some of these men and women must have trembled when making this act of rebellion. Yet they knew what they did. Their teachers had told them how Christ had fought against these powers and principalities and how he had won victory over them. . . . each convert stepped into the cross. Three times he was in a dramatic way buried in the water of the cross-baptistry. A presbyter asked: "Do you believe in God the Father Almighty?" "Do you believe in Christ Jesus, the Son of God . . .?" "Do you believe in the Holy Spirit, in the Holy Church, and the resurrection of the flesh?" "I believe" said each convert. . . . In their baptism the converts of Rhodes were taken into the death and life of Christ, into his struggle and victory. From now on they were no more to be puppets for powers and principalitites to play with. . . . From now on they and all who are baptized are incorporated into Christ's army, into the *militia Christi* for the struggle of faith. . . . The bishop laid his hand on the converts and prayed the following significant prayer: "O God . . . make them worthy to be filled with Thy Holy Spirit and send upon them Thy Holy Spirit and send upon them Thy grace, that they may serve Thee according to Thy will. . . . " Then the bishop anointed them and thus they were fully taken into God's people.[5]

Trust and loyalty are not separate in the life of a believer; they intertwine. Neither are they static; they develop over the years. A clear illustration of this growing interrelationship is found in the life of Sherwood Eddy, one of the pioneers of the Student Christian Movement. As a young man before the turn of the century, Eddy accepted Christ as his personal savior. At that time he understood God's cause to be the personal salvation of others in his own town. Not long after, catching a vision of God's love for all persons, he went to India in the cause of world missions. He was one of that notable company who espoused the motto "The Evangelization of the World in This Generation." However, as the years passed, he felt increasingly frustrated about his relation to God and about his service to God. Listen to his description of the discovery of a deeper and more satisfying experience of confidence than he had ever known.

I was bitter, discouraged, rebellious. I still believed there was a God but that I had missed the way, and one morning, after a sleepless night, I cried to God to show me the way out. And then in the dawn of a new truth, one simple word changed life forever. . . . Paraphrased it might read: "Whoever drinks of the waters of this earth will thirst again." They do not satisfy— wealth, pleasure, power, ambition, knowledge, the world, the flesh—"but whoever drinks and keeps drinking of the water of life that I shall give him shall never thirst again." . . . Something happened that day thirty years ago, and it has been happening ever since. . . . Thenceforth, the eternal God was my refuge and underneath were the everlasting arms . . . and I believe that I shall never thirst again.

Shortly after this deepening of his trust came a broadening of his understanding of God's cause and of his own loyalty to it. It took place about the time of World War I. He writes:

I saw the world rent and divided in industrial, racial and international strife—a world of sordid materialism, autocratic exploitation and organized militarism, ever preparing for further war. Had I a philosophy of life or a message equal to this whole world's need? . . . Had I a gospel big enough to meet the need of this warring world and this unjust social order? In seeking a solution I turned back to study Jesus' way of life, in the simple love of God and one's neighbor. . . . Now there broke upon me the first gleams of a social gospel that sought not only to save individuals for the future, but here and now in this world of bitter need, to christianize the whole of life and all its relationships—industrial, social, sexual, racial, international. As I had once seen Christ identified with the need of distant pagan lands, I saw him now, hungry and athirst, naked, sick and in prison, in the pagan practices and the blighted lives of our own social order.[6]

The record of Eddy's faith pilgrimage is important. It not only shows the twin realities of trust and loyalty, but also indicates how over time changes may emerge in the structure of one's faith relationship. It is important to remember that faith as trust does not always deepen, nor does faith as loyalty always broaden in its concept of God's work in the world. Regretfully the opposite can be true—some lose confidence in God and narrow their understanding of his purpose to the confines of their own soul.

## Implications for Evangelism

By the examples above we have sought to make plain some of what is meant when faith is referred to as a relational act consisting of both trust and loyalty. The limited data provided by these cases certainly does not exhaust the ways Christian persons trust God or the ways in which they express their loyalty to him; these are as varied as his goodness and as broad as his purpose for the human family.

Following this discussion it is proper to ask, "What do we learn from the understanding of faith as trust and loyalty for the work of evangelism?"

1. Faith as trust and faith as loyalty must receive equal stress in the work of evangelism.

To evangelize is to invite persons to trust the love and mercy of Christ. To evangelize is to ask persons to place themselves under the sovereignty of Christ as loyal subjects. To emphasize loyalty without trust or trust without loyalty is to offer a truncated half-relationship to Christ.

Unfortunately in current evangelistic practice, faith as trust is stressed in a way that too often obscures faith as loyalty. When this is done, we are guilty of holding out what Dietrich Bonhoeffer has called "cheap grace":

> Cheap grace is the preaching of forgiveness without requiring repentance, baptism without church discipline, communion without confession, absolution without personal confession. Cheap grace is grace without discipleship, grace without the cross. . . .[7]

Thus it is that many persons receive the consolations of faith as trust in Christ the Savior but do not participate in any serious way in the ongoing work of Christ the Lord. They are beneficiaries of

those who espoused the cause in other times but give no promise
of contributing to a legacy of faith or hope or love in this or
succeeding generations. In part at least, this is what Presbyterian
Leighton Ford, a protege of Billy Graham, seemed to have been
working on when, after prison riots in New York, his altar calls
included not only an appeal to accept Christ as Savior but to
serve Christ by undertaking some aspect of prison reform.
Translating this to the congregational setting, it might mean that
all new members, young and old, would be given challenges for
participation in God's work in church and world. United Methodist George Hunter suggests that there should be a clear call for
specific, not generalized, commitments to Christ, e.g. by working
with the elderly, visiting in hospitals, tutoring school dropouts,
teaching church school, calling on newcomers, working for
adequate housing and health care, etc. In our evangelistic appeals
we can let persons glimpse God's total work in the world. They
can be introduced in person or by reading to those whose vision
of serving God includes both personal and social dimensions.
With such models in mind they will be better able to respond to
the call of Christ the Lord.

2. A person's need and capacity for faith as trust and faith as
loyalty varies throughout a lifetime.

The better educational and evangelistic materials being produced for American denominations wisely ask that we try to
understand in some depth the persons to whom we would
communicate good news. While we know that a full-bodied faith
consists of trust and loyalty, our perception of a person's special
needs at a certain place in the life cycle will lead us to emphasize
those aspects of the faith relationship that are most appropriate.
To a child our main stress likely would be on faith as trust.
However, for mid-teens we will be remiss in our call to faith if the
dimension of loyalty to Kingdom work is not given stress. In
extreme old age, especially when one's powers are waning, the
emphasis might well return to trust. Nonetheless, there will be
variations in every individual's experience.

Martin Niemoeller, a vigorously active anti-Nazi pastor, wrote
from prison, "I used to carry the gospel; now the gospel carries

me." The first statement refers to a time in life when he served as a loyal partner with God in an effort to avert the horrors of the Third Reich; the latter takes note of his new status as a dependent captive who receives trustfully and gratefully the goodness of God's love and care. Sherwood Eddy, we have seen, burned himself out in faith as loyalty. It was only as he tapped the spiritual nutrients that flowed from a trustful relation with the Savior that he was able to continue and then expand his service to Christ in the world.

An authentic evangelism will call for full faith in Christ which is trustful of his grace and loyal to his service. It will do this in ways that are appropriate to the needs and respectful of the rights of each person.

### FOR FURTHER REFLECTION

1. To emphasize faith as trust in Christ seems innocent enough. John Wesley in his Journal wrote a letter to his brother in which he indicates that much opposition came to him because he preached faith alone for salvation.

I have seen upon this occasion, more than ever I could have imagined, how intolerable the doctrine of faith is to the mind of man; and how peculiarly intolerable to religious men. One may say the most unchristian things, even down to Deism; the most enthusiastic things, so they proceed but upon mental raptures, lights and unions; the most severe things, even the whole rigour of ascetic mortification; and all this will be forgiven. But if you speak of faith in such a manner as makes Christ a Savior to the utmost, a most universal help and refuge; in such a manner as takes away glorying, but adds happiness to wretched man; as discovers a greater pollution in the best of us, than we could before acknowledge, but brings a greater deliverance from it than we could before expect; if any one offers to talk at this rate, he shall be heard with the same abhorrence as if he was going to rob mankind of their salvation.[8]

2. In recent years Billy Graham has been putting more emphasis on the cost of discipleship. He continues to stress that we are saved by grace, but makes it clear that discipleship means making Christ the Lord of our daily lives and spelling out the cost of following Christ.

How do you relate this to the trust and loyalty understanding of faith?

Can a congregation that really needs new members afford to talk about the demands of the gospel? Is your congregation "soft" or "hard" on the issue of faith as loyalty? What can be done to change this?

3. Is faith as trust in some ways more important than faith as loyalty? A person argued that it is—"Our capacity for trust comes first in life, trust in God corresponds more nearly with our fundamental needs for safety, love, and esteem, and Scripture seems to give dominant emphasis to faith as trust." What do you think? If trust must be given priority, does that mean that faith as loyalty can be deemphasized?

4. When it comes to faith as loyalty, people have different opinions about what it means to serve God. Is it important that all Christians be in agreement on what loyalty to God's cause means? Are there some ways in which you would expect all Christians to be loyal to Christ? List some of these ways. Should these be made plain to persons considering becoming Christians? Is there room in the church for diversity on what obedience to Christ work may mean? In chapter 6 the chart entitled "How God Works in the World Through His People" indicates some of the different ways Christians have felt called to serve Christ. Could your congregation tolerate that much diversity? Why would you?

5. Dr. Bonhoeffer, the German theologian of the Nazi era, once counseled that if a person could not believe he should obey, if he could not obey he should believe. This seems to be a recognition of the fact that we Christians oscillate between faith/trust (believing) and faith/loyalty (obedience). Is this part of your experience? Do you think his advice would help our Christian growth? Do you see any implications in his words for the work of evangelism?

6. In this chapter and chapter 1 we read of two persons who burned themselves out in faith/loyalty. Reread the Sherwood Eddy and Edith Black stories. Is this similar to what is meant when busy church people speak of having "organizational fatigue"? How can we help ourselves and others keep a good balance between giving ourselves in faith/loyalty and sustaining ourselves by faith/trust?

7. For a person to have both faith/trust and faith/loyalty in some cause or god seems to be essential for proper human growth. In chapter 5 the sections on faith style of infancy and adolescence speak to this issue from the perspective of developmental psychologist Erik Erikson. You might find it helpful to scan this material now.

8. Trust and loyalty as aspects of faith are often stressed in hymns. Flip through the hymnal to pick out those which stress faith as loyalty, e.g. "Take My Life and Let It Be (Consecrated Lord to Thee)" or faith as trust, e.g. "Be Still My Soul"—or both equally, e.g. "Trust and Obey."

# 4 | *Faith as a Personal Act*

In chapters 2 and 3 we have seen that an evangelism worthy of the name will present faith as a dynamic relationship centered in Christ which calls for both trust and loyalty.

In this chapter we investigate the proposition that a true evangelism will present faith in Christ in a manner that encourages a proper respect for each person's freedom of choice.

As our "text" we use words of C. S. Lewis, Cambridge professor, renowned author, and Christian apologist, who came to faith in mid-life.

In his spiritual autobiography, *Surprised by Joy,* his conversion to theism is described as one major step toward his conversion to Christianity. He was going up Headington Hill on top of a bus. Of his inner experience he writes:

> I felt myself, there and then, given a free choice. I could open the door or keep it shut. . . . Neither choice was presented as a duty; no threat or promise. . . . I chose to open . . . yet it did not really seem possible to do the opposite. . . .[1]

Let's now examine his words.

## Deliberation

"I felt myself, there and then, given a free choice. I could open the door or keep it shut." A choice between alternatives was set before him—agnosticism or theism. Inwardly the question was, "Shall I choose this course or that?" His circumstance was not unlike that of Robert Frost's traveler:

Two roads diverged in a yellow wood,
and sorry I could not travel both
And be one traveler, long I stood
And looked down one as far as I could
To where it bent in the undergrowth . . .[2]

When confronted with such alternatives, one ordinarily begins a process of deliberation.

To deliberate means literally to weigh. It involves a mental balancing of the reasons for and against particular options. It is the act of sizing up the advantages and consequences of one course of action in contrast to another. The process of deliberating may be of long or short duration. The Lewis account as printed here makes his period of deliberation seem brief indeed. However, a reading of the context from which this quotation is taken shows that some thought preceded his faith decision.

Invitations to faith are in effect calls to select from among alternatives. Two illustrations from the Bible will help make this plain:

Now therefore fear the LORD, and serve him in sincerity and in faithfulness; put away the gods which your fathers served beyond the River, and in Egypt, and serve the LORD. . . . Choose this day whom you will serve, whether the gods your fathers served in the region beyond the River, or the gods of the Amorites in whose land you dwell; but as for me and my house, we will serve the LORD.

(Joshua 24:14–15)

In a similar way Jesus called his disciples to make up their minds:

And passing along by the Sea of Galilee, he saw Simon and Andrew the brother of Simon casting a net in the sea; for they were fishermen. And Jesus said to them, "Follow me and I will make you become fishers of men."

(Mark 1:16–17)

Both passages imply that other gods or leaders could be chosen. Before answering, those who heard these calls to faith had to make serious considerations. They doubtless pondered and assessed the credentials of the caller as well as the implications for their lives. In our world there are countless calls to faith. We live in an age of "over-choice." Religious merchants are hawking their wares on every corner: Transcendental Meditation, Humanism, Hare Krishna, Satanism, Technology, Hassidism, Unification Church, Scientology, Communism, Islam, Zen Buddhism, Super Patriotism, Children of God, Theosophy. Many adherents of these and other faith options are "evangelistic" in their appeals—they are out to make converts. As Christians we, too, are "sellers" in the open market. Nor is there reason for us to be hesitant in commending the Christian alternative to life's deepest issues. Scripture and our experience of life in Christ equip us to demonstrate and explain this way.

As we do so, however, efforts should be made to encourage and assist persons in deliberating on their various options—read about them, discuss them, compare them, share in the life of some groups, evaluate them and finally make their own free choice among them. Christian faith, chosen after careful deliberation among various options, will be strong and steady over the long haul. Shortcutting this procedure or rushing persons into premature decisions may produce fair-weather Christians. Christian faith, chosen after careful weighing of alternatives, probably has the best chance of being strong and durable.

**Indoctrination**

"Neither choice was presented as a duty; no threat or promise. . . ." Lewis is telling us that he was not coerced—no pressures from parents or peers, no threats of academic banishment, no promises of social approval. The dark background of his words is the fact that many a person's search for faith is so encumbered.

When one's aim is to bring persons to faith in Christ, it is an easy temptation to use ignoble "means" for its achievement. The history of evangelism in America reveals one debate after another about the propriety of particular "means"—what today we call "methods" of evangelism. Some have debased evangelism to the point that they will use virtually any method which gets affirmative response. However, a large concern of ours should be whether a particular method or approach is fair to persons. Does it leave room for faith as a free choice among alternatives? Church school classes, visitation programs, communicant and confirmation groups, revival meetings, and other approaches to faith awakening need to be examined with this question in mind.

In the end the question for evangelism is: "Can we have strongly committed congregations which at the same time have sufficient openness to allow for and encourage the personal character of Christian faith?" The answer can be "yes" if the issue of indoctrination is recognized and resolved.

Indoctrination is "the attempt to authoritatively and unquestioningly impose on others beliefs and belief systems whose acceptance really should be rooted in the agent's own free and rational choice."[3] The Amish practice an extreme form of religious indoctrination. They refuse to send their children beyond elementary school because they believe, doubtless correctly, that too much knowledge of alternate lifestyles and too much development of the capacity for critical thought will undermind their community of faith. Even when they teach the Bible within their own circle, no discussion or question concerning it is allowed. Unfortunately, too many Christians feel that their God-given call is to "protect" persons from knowledge of other alternatives and thus from free choice itself.

What we need and, if we work at it, what we can have is a non-indoctrinating evangelism. Here a response of faith in Christ is clearly sought without any effort to suppress the autonomy of the individual. Too often our evangelization is not for faith but for domestication—that is, its aim is to transfer religious knowledge to a person and to secure conformity to some existing religious order. Evangelization for faith would be that which seeks to heighten a person's understanding, intentionality and consciousness toward God in Christ. It would begin by encouraging a free act of faith and have as its long range hope a free person in Christ.

Several years ago an article in a national magazine was illustrated with an oversized, realistic clenched fist from which the arms and legs of a struggling man protruded. By contrast, a bulletin cover at Sage Chapel at Cornell University once carried an abstract but recognizable symbol of an open hand, palm up; nestled in it a tender green sprout representative of a person was growing. Human organizations can be to their members as either of these hands—suppressive of personal growth, or conducive to the self's free development. In the words of Harvard's Gordon Allport, we should hope that every congregation will strive to be "an affiliative structure that does not retard, but frees one to become a child of God"[4]—not a child of *our* doctrine or *our* religious institution.

### Decision

"I chose to open. . . ." He made a self-conscious decision. A solution that put an end to wavering and uncertainty had been reached. For Lewis agnosticism was a thing of the past; he chose instead the personal God of theism.

To decide puts an end to vascillating between options. It cuts off debate. One course of action or way of thinking is selected; others are rejected. In marriage "yes" is said to one person; "no" to others. Having made that choice, one's life is forever different. In every sphere of life, one's choices are equally fateful. As the wayfarer in Frost's poem saw it:

> I shall be telling this with a sigh
> Somewhere ages and ages hence:
> Two roads diverged in a wood, and I—
> I took the one less traveled by,
> And that has made all the difference.[5]

In New Testament terms the difference is between light and darkness, life and death, the Kingdom of God and the kingdoms of this world. Choosing freely from among alternatives is an essential part of what is meant by an act of faith. Being brought up in a Christian family and in church is often a good preparation for faith, but no one is a Christian until, and unless, he or she has made a personal decision to follow Christ and to accept his love. Living in a country with many Christian values embedded in its folkways and laws may be of help when it comes to practicing the Christian way in the affairs of daily life—nonetheless, no person may be said to have Christian faith until he or she has self-consciously chosen to trust Christ and advance his cause.

Even the best endowments of home and country do not guarantee that we will have faith. Faith is *our* response to what God has done in Jesus Christ. We do not have to be Christians, but if we are it must be because we—no one else—decided freely to place our ultimate trust and highest loyalty in the God of the Father of Jesus Christ.

As Christians we hope very much that persons will decide to have faith in Christ. William H. McElveen of the Moravian Church has written an evangelism guide for his congregation. One section on "Enabling Persons to Make a Decision" has good counsel for us all.

The ultimate decision we seek is that persons commit their life to God in Jesus Christ in the Church. We do not apologize for that for we feel it is a good decision for anyone and everyone to make. At the same time, however, it is very inappropriate and wrong to ask a person to make that kind of commitment without knowing what it means.

When we present a choice or decision to a person, we must be very sure that we give the person both the freedom and the responsibility for making that decision himself. If we make it for him or put pressure on him to make the decision in a particular way that may please us, we are denying him a vital part of the good possibilities we are encouraging him to accept.

With the decision of faith we begin the Christian journey. None of us understands enough about Christ and God or even about ourselves to make such a choice with full knowledge; yet it is never made without knowledge. Bishop Stephen Neill of India used to invite persons to make this beginning affirmation: "I commit as much as I know of myself to as much as I know of God in Christ." That is good advice for us and a good word to speak to those we hope will make a decision of faith. It delivers us and them from the presumption of pretending more than we know. It makes decision possible for many persons who otherwise might hold back.

**Paradox**

" . . . Yet it did not really seem possible to do the opposite." With this cryptic comment, C. S. Lewis tempers his emphasis on free choice. In context it puts a very proper damper on the bravado of any who overly exalt the role of human freedom in the act of faith.

The "conversion" statement of Lewis, which we have been probing, occurs in a chapter which he entitled "Checkmate." In it he speaks of four "Moves"—capital M—against himself. Upon examination the "Moves" turn out to be his reading of Euripides' *Hippolytus,* Alexander's *Space, Time and Deity,* Chesterton's *Everlasting Man,* and several offhand comments made by friends, both atheist and Christian. Finally, at the end of the chapter, he speaks of his coming to faith as the result of the compulsion or "checkmate" of God. Thus, on the one hand, he can speak of what sounds like his complete freedom of choice while, on the other hand, he can speak of God compelling him to believe.

In the Lewis experience we discover the paradox of faith— man's freedom and the gracious working of God's Holy Spirit. As we have seen, it is God who opens the door of faith (Acts 14:27). Yet, in the New Testament, faith is presented as a choice set before us: "If anyone hears my voice and opens the door, I will come in to him" (Revelations 3:20).

This seeming contradiction, so characteristic of Christian experience, was well stated in a proposed Presbyterian confession:

> God invites us to put our trust in Christ. He leads us to abandon our old way of life and to adopt Christ's way. We are awesomely responsible for this decision and have the fearful ability to say no to God. But when we have trusted and repented we see very clearly that God's Holy Spirit worked this in us.

The emphasis on faith as a more-than-human action has deep

roots within the Christian tradition. For example, Martin Luther, who understood faith as a lively, reckless confidence in the grace of God, stressed that it was not something we could fetch up on our own—not something we can dredge up from our imagination; it is rather God's work in us.

What is being said here is in sharp contrast to the opening pages of this chapter with the emphasis on faith as an individual's response. Now we see the wider perspective of the divine milieu—Christian faith is God's gift. This is so in at least two ways: 1. In the sense that God gives himself in Christ as the object of faith. 2. In the sense that God works in our lives by the Holy Spirit to evoke our faith in him. Were it not for God's gracious activity past and present, there would be no Christian faith.

How is such a faith relationship possible? On one hand, as we have been saying, it is possible because we *choose* to place our trust in and give our loyalty to God. Yet, the ordinary human disposition toward him is one of disbelief or distrust; our will to believe in Christ seems incapacitated. Therefore Christian theology insists that faith is only possible because in our separation God himself comes to us (Romans 5:6–11). He interrupts our self-centeredness, fearfulness, and defensiveness. Through Jesus Christ he restores our ability to trust him and inspires our capacity to be loyal to him. In union with Christ a new confidence about ourselves, the world, and God is born; in Christ our narrow loyalties are enlarged so that self, family, church, nation find their rightful places within the universal sphere of the Kingdom of our Lord and his Christ. Faith is possible because God in Christ is reconciling the world to himself (2 Corinthians 5:11–21) and because his Holy Spirit is abroad in our world (1 Corinthians 2:6–13).

The implication for those concerned to awaken faith in others should be plain. We are to work to enable persons to make a decision of faith. But, we work with God. Our role, though essential, is relatively modest. From one perspective a medical doctor plays a highly significant part in the prenatal care and delivery of a child. Viewed in another way, a doctor is only an assistant in a process set in motion and brought to climax by forces over which there is little or no control. So of faith, its conception and birth are not of our doing; yet, by God's call, we do have a part to play in its emergence and growth.

Having analyzed faith as a personal, relational, and centered act, we can now state three criteria which may be used in either planning or evaluating evangelism efforts.

## The Criteria of Faith in Evangelism

1. Evangelism will present Jesus Christ as Faith's Center.
2. Evangelism will present faith as a dynamic relationship to Christ which calls for both trust and loyalty.
3. Evangelism will present faith in Christ in a manner that encourages a free choice from among alternatives.

### FOR FURTHER REFLECTION

1. Some people seem to go to extremes not to influence the religious views of others. Parents have been heard to say, "We don't take our children to church because we want them to be free to choose their own religion when they grow up."

   Can you give several reasons to support their view? Do some parents go to the opposite extreme? What is a healthy balance between too little and too much influence?

2. As a loyal Christian, Charles Schultz, creator of "Peanuts," once wrote:

   I refuse to go out and speak to groups as a so-called celebrity, because I think anyone who becomes religious because somebody else is religious is already on the wrong track. A person should be converted because he has seen the figure of Jesus and has been inspired by him. And this is the only thing that makes a person a Christian.[6]

   What do you think of this statement? Is that good advice for him only? With what in his statement do you agree, disagree?

3. Congregations regularly receive members. How can our procedures for seeking and enrolling new persons (youth and adults) in our fellowship be improved? How can we encourage a faith that is centered in Christ, in which both trust and loyalty are present, and that is freely chosen?

The results of your thinking on this might well be reported for consideration to the governing board of your church. A letter to your denominational headquarters will likely bring some good counsel on how to make membership more meaningful.

4. If faith is a gift of God, why should we worry about doing evangelism at all? Isn't the advice of those who opposed the early Protestant missionary movement nearly correct: "If God wants to convert the heathen, he'll do it himself!"? From the point of view of Scripture, how could those persons argue that this was the right view? How could it be argued that it is the wrong view?

5. Since evangelism is a cooperative effort between God, the evangelist, and the person to be reached, prayer ought to play a large part in our efforts at faith awakening. Here is a plan called "intercessory evangelism" which a pastor proposed to his congregation. You might consider encouraging similar commitment in your church.

---

### MY COMMITMENT

1. I will seek to discover one person whose faith in Christ is non-existent or weak.                        \_\_\_\_\_

2. I will pray that that person will come to have an increase of trust and loyalty in the Lord.                \_\_\_\_\_

3. I will follow God's leading about whether or not I should talk to him personally.                          \_\_\_\_\_

4. I will seek to deepen and strengthen my own faith in God through prayer.                                    \_\_\_\_\_

---

6. An articulate layman well beyond his three score years and ten reacted to this chapter in a way that focuses a great deal of feelings on its point about freedom. A good discussion and debate could be planned using his comments.

I couldn't disagree more with the philosophy prevalent in the world today of *complete freedom of choice*. I know, of course, that as of now it is called educationally sound. But it is the reason also for the condition the world finds itself in. It is the reason the Catholic Church is losing membership and effectiveness. It is the reason the Protestant Church is not as influential as formerly. It is the reason that youth is in turmoil. It caused Watergate. It causes crime. C. S. Lewis was at least mature, well read, etc. Some reason for freedom of choice maybe—with most there is not enough knowledge to make choices—they must be guided and influenced, especially the young.

7. Most of us would be against an indoctrinating form of evangelism. But what would a non-indoctrinating form look like? One of the best guides is: *Evangelism: Person to Person,* from the Presbyterian Church, U.S. The following outline of its main points reflects its spirit.
   a. We will go to persons where they are, with understanding and Christian love.
   b. We will listen to what that person has to say.
   c. We will be natural and honest.
   d. We will present the gospel of love lovingly.
   e. We will help him to clarify his situation.
   f. We want the person to make the decision for himself.
   g. We will go in faith.

8. To talk as this chapter does about the importance of personal decision seems to point to some specific time when a person commits his or her life to Christ. What does this imply about those church members who can recollect no specific time of decision for Christ. These selections from an interview with Billy Graham may aid reflection on this:

   *If a young person does not have a spiritual experience they can point to, does that mean that they're not somehow quite in tune yet?*

   Not at all, because I believe that we're not to base our faith on experience alone. We're to base it on the Word of God also. The two work together.

   *There are those who feel that there is no one time when they have been saved. You support this feeling?*

   I *certainly* do. Many people cannot point to the day nor the hour that they've made their commitment to Christ. They've always loved him. They almost grew up with Christ. And I feel that I'm very fortunate that I can remember. Maybe God saw that I needed that experience to strengthen my faith in years to come, that I needed that moment I could point to when I could say "Yes, this is where I met Christ."[7]

# 5 | Readiness for Faith

When are the capacities for faith as a personal, relational, centered act available to the self? When can one choose in a relatively free manner? When is one capable of placing confidence in, and offering fidelity to, another who is greater? When is a person competent to discriminate among those objects which beckon for his/her trust and loyalty? These are questions with which any authentic nurture and evangelism must be concerned.

Faith, we know, is a free gift of God, but it is given in accordance with the laws of human growth. By saying this we are not trying to reduce religion or faith to a psychological explanation or to suggest that psychological factors rigidly determine a person's religious faith. Our aim is much less pretentious. We are searching for hints and clues in the writings of some psychologists of human development in order better to understand when a person is ready for a response of faith.

We all know that there are educational approaches suitable for persons at elementary, secondary, and college levels. In the same way there are evangelistic approaches that fit better at one stage of life than another; this is due to the fact that our capacity or readiness for faith seems to change with the years. As we anticipate development in other subject matter areas, we should expect and provide opportunities for growth in the sphere of religion and faith. The aim here is to assist in discovering appropriate ways of awakening and nurturing the faith of persons of various ages.[1]

## The Faith Style of Infancy

Everyone of us has inhabited the world of infancy; yet from the beginning it has been to us as a hidden, unexplored continent. Only within the last decades have we begun successfully to chart its mysteries. The child, we have learned, is not only a bundle of physiological needs but possesses as well a rich and rapidly expanding emotional and intellectual life. Moreover, many now believe, following the lead of Erik Erikson, that faith as trust has its rottage in the first experiences of life.[2]

During this period—which is a time of taking in, receiving, and incorporating—Erikson holds that infants will develop within themselves some mixture of basic trust and mistrust. A successful negotiation of this phase implies that trust outweighs distrust. Though residues of both are inevitable and even necessary, the exact outcome of this stage will be determined by the quality of the care delivered to infants by trustworthy parental persons. If infants are smiled at, cuddled, played with, if their needs are met when they arise and discomforts quickly removed, then, in Erikson's view, they will develop a sense of trust in the world as a safe place and of people as dependable. If the opposite is true, the ratio of mistrust will rise accordingly. While mistrust is primarily maladaptive, it is not entirely so, for mistrust allows one to sense and to anticipate discomfort in future situations. Too much mistrust will leave a residue of alienation and estrangement in the life of the person. Whatever the amalgam of trust and mistrust, it will be transferred into later stages and, if basic trust is not in the ascendance, an attitude of fear and suspicion, abandonment and deprivation carry over toward the world and people.

The task of child rearing—feeding, diaper changing, walking the baby in what W. Jack Lewis used to call the "wee-wee hours of the morning"—does not in itself appear to be religious. But surely a church which hopes adults will trust God as Divine Provider will not fail to note or to encourage the preparatory— what we may call pre-evangelistic—responsibilities of parents with young children. Erikson offers good counsel to the Christian community when he writes: "Whosoever says that he has religion must derive a faith from it which is transmitted to infants in the form of basic trust."[3]

If all of this is true, or even approximately so, our congregations will be well advised to give increased educational and emotional support to the families of young children. Parents rightly need to understand the general stewardship of child rearing, but more specifically they must be led to see the relationship of their parental faithfulness or lack thereof to the capacity of the child to trust the world in general and God in particular. In the act of infant baptism or dedication, we both claim and testify that his grace is sufficient for parent and child and congregation.

## The Faith Style of Early Childhood

Young children of this period are very observant and imitative of the faith activity—church-going, praying, singing, etc.—of those closest to them. Their limited experience, cognitive ability, and capacity for spontaneous and sometimes fantastic reinterpretation of what they see and hear may cause them to have incorrect ideas or mixed-up notions about God, Jesus, Santa Claus, fairies, preachers, etc.

Those familiar with the work of Jean Piaget on cognitive growth will recognize that we are discussing children in the pre-operational stage, ages two to seven, whose thought tends to be fanciful and illogical. Piaget's research for the most part has been concerned with the child's understanding of physical reality, mathematics, and logic. He has not studied religious thinking. Are his conclusions applicable in this field? Careful work done in England a decade ago by Ronald Goldman demonstrated that it is.

Goldman's research, reported in the volume *Religious Thinking from Childhood to Adolescence,* seeks to answer one basic question: How does the child at various stages of development understand and interpret religious concepts and symbols such as those found in the biblical narratives? In his conclusion he offers this summary about the thinking of young children concerning God:

God at this stage of development is conceived in physical anthropomorphic terms, as an old man in Palestinian clothes, with a physical voice and presence, living in heaven, which is situated in the sky, making occasional visits in person to the earth. His visitations are rare nowadays as compared with Bible times. He is unpredictable in his actions, rather like a touchy, powerful adult and sometimes vindictive to those who are naughty. His powers are akin to those of a magician and he is to be feared for this reason.[4]

Another feature of this period is that children can be taught to repeat virtually any religious language that adults teach them—commandments, creeds, catechisms, etc. The documentary movie *Marjoe*—showing a four- or five-year-old child "preacher" delivering sermons, praying and performing weddings—provides a vivid example of this early capacity for memorization and repetition of the most profound biblical and theological words. However, because of children's limited experience of life and undeveloped cognitive structure, their interpretations of religious concepts are at first confused and illogical, and then utterly literal and concrete and more often than not without comprehension of the inner or spiritual meaning of the words used.

All this does not mean that the child's efforts are of no avail, nor does it mean that the religious values and behavior of parents are of no consequence. Although wise parents will recognize that full Christian faith (as a centered, relational, personal act) is beyond the capacity of young children, they will not fail to see that faith in a limited way is present and that the first years are an important time of preparation for a mature decision of faith.

Paul Tillich says of his own parental conditioning: "The importance of such parental legacies is not that they determine the course of one's life, but that they define the scope and supply the substance out of which critical decisions are drawn."[5]

Another writer whose name is unknown wrote what can only be called a magnificient tribute to his parental legacy:

My parents really did nothing about religious education, at least I don't think that they ever consciously saw themselves as concerned with it.
But I felt that each as sincerely as the other loved Jesus

Christ very much and lived by his grace and for his kingdom. As a child you want nothing better than to share in all these things; you see how fine it all is, how happy it makes you, how real it is.

For me and all my brothers and sisters the living faith of our parents was decisive.[6]

These words push beyond all worrisome thoughts of the intellectual incapacity of children to a vision of the high and hopeful calling of Christian parenthood. The child's faith is not all that it can be, but in its season it is adequate; with proper encouragement it holds promise of later flowering.

## The Faith Style of Childhood

Children continue to be dependent on those closest to them. They look to adults around them for faith as well as food.

A typical question of a person at this stage is, "What do we believe?" Such persons are usually glad to accept from someone of authority—parent, minister, teacher—statements of "our" doctrine or instructions about the way "we" do things. They have a strong sense of belonging and a glad sense of sharing a common faith. Conformity to group expectations and dependence upon the beliefs and values of others in one's church characterize this faith style. Critical questioning and doubting are virtually absent. When mental difficulties arise persons at this period try to harmonize their own life experience with the teachings of their religious group. If there is a conflict between the two, they think the problem is in themselves rather than in the belief system. During this period one's loyalty and trust are clearly dependent upon significant adults in family and congregation.

Children will vary in their capacity to rightly handle the various stories of the Bible and teachings of the church. The religious thinking of late juniors and pre-adolescents is described by Goldman in the following way:

This is the time between fantasy and adult logic, when some confusion is apparent and a great deal of intellectual activity is taking place. In religious terms, the picture is something like the following. Cruder anthropomorphic ideas of God are receding and the emphasis is much more upon supernatural than superhuman concepts of the deity. Some limiting human elements still persist in that God still has a human voice of physical quality and possesses power seen in physical and magical terms. There is a great deal of confusion as a child tries to think his way through these problems. For example, God if present must still be present himself in person, and concepts of omnipresence are still uncertain.[7]

Our parental anxiety and our proper concern to pass on the Christian faith to our children lead during this period to a wide variety of educational approaches, especially through the church school. Unfortunately, a limited number of adults wrongheadedly view childhood as the best time to press for an "adult" profession of faith. Such "child evangelism," whether utilizing revivals, confirmation classes, or the church school, has a long tradition in America going back to the eighteenth century. If faith is, as we have described it, a personal, relational, and centered act, and if developmental studies are even approximately correct, the capacity for "full" faith is not available to the average child. This does not mean that the children are bereft of God's grace in Christ. It only means that they are not yet able consciously to comprehend that grace or with full purpose to commit themselves to it. Our task, as the child's congregation, parents, and friends is to provide all the means of grace (prayer, worship, communion, Bible study, fellowship opportunities) against the day when the child, grown more toward adult years, can choose freely and knowingly to trust Christ and render loyal service to him.

Children at this stage of life obviously have faith, and it is often impressive to behold, but it can best be understood as a borrowed faith, as mainly "secondhand," not "firsthand." Typically, persons come to their own faith in adolescent years or beyond.

Rose Kennedy in *Times to Remember* puts all this wisely.

Nor should we think of faith either as something we are born into, a kind of family legacy in the spiritual realm. Although we teach our children very early in life what we call the truths of faith, each one of them at some time in his or her development as a human being must pray for the gift of faith, must personally accept the gift of faith and cherish it as his or her own.[8]

Most often this praying for and personally accepting faith takes place during the years of youth.

## The Faith Style of Youth

Adolescence brings new powers of body, spirit, and mind. It is a time of new ways of looking at and conceiving the world. Young people at this period can think about ideal families and religions and compare them with "imperfect" families and religions. Critical thinking begins to dawn. Problems can be formulated with more clarity, alternatives explored and tested. For many this period of life marks the onset of what Piaget calls "formal operations"—the highest level of cognitive ability.

In the sphere of religion the young person begins to emerge from the parental and congregational womb toward a faith life of his/her own. There is movement away from "our faith" toward a quest for "my faith." On occasion, the transitions of this period seem natural and easy; at other times they are painful and traumatic. Two personal reminiscences by young adults provide helpful insight.

1. *Young Adult A:*
My faith did not arrive full-grown. Its beginnings fade back into the vague memories of childhood—church, family, my own prayers, religious instruction. I grew consciously in personal relationship to God during early adolescence when I learned to read Scripture (primarily the Gospels) in a listening, pondering way, and to respond in prayer, conversing with Christ, the Father, or the Spirit.

My faith-relationship with God has been consistently both mediated and direct. Others inspire me, teach me, encourage me, allow me to enter into their relationship to God (in discussion or in prayer), or help me to clarify my own feelings toward God. And in individual prayer and in the interiorness of my own consciousness as I live my life, God and I have grown immediately closer together.

2. *Young Adult B:*
Three years ago, I was just entering a liberal arts college and during my first semester I took a course in "Religion and Culture" and a course in "Religion in the Developing Personali-

ty." I brought to this academic experience a background of thorough-going fundamentalism. At the end of this semester I had devastated both courses and proclaimed my weariness of the religious life as I knew and understood it. This clash of funamentalist theology with a study of the phenomenology of religion that occurred in the classroom precipitated a quest for a meaningful faith in terms of my own critical self-awareness. . . . I was so accepting of the norms up to this point that I could not see myself as a person outside of the family and church structure. My identity was bound by a particular system of beliefs. This was so much the case that I never thought to ask how effective the church was in terms of meeting my psychological and intellectual needs. It was almost as if I did not have the right to question the sacredness of all that I had been taught by the church. . . . The religion professors whom I was studying under at this time became, for me, representatives of possible ideological options. This was of critical importance. I sensed where I wanted to go in terms of religious and faith development, but I needed live models. These models had to supply: (1) answers to intellectual questions about the meaning of faith; (2) intuitive insight into where I was and where I wanted to be in order to help me sharpen my perspective and articulate my aims; and (3) a lifestyle that exemplified the life of faith and the responsibilities inherent in that life. I count myself fortunate that my models were to be found among the faithful.

For some the challenge of college years may result in a radical relativism and abandonment of faith altogether. For others it may prove to be a transitional period on the way to a more mature appropriation of one's earlier faith. The way persons go may be influenced in part by the extent to which early and present models—parents, pastors, teachers, friends in church—lived up to their faith. If upon reflection the persons feel the models were "faking it" or didn't really mean it, it may be easy for them to abandon faith. Unfortunately, too many have been given what they consider valid grounds for such rejection.

The capacity for faith/loyalty comes to the fore in these years.

Erikson's discussions of identity and fidelity offer considerable insight into this new readiness.

The fifth stage in the Eriksonian vision of the human life cycle concerns the sense of identity. Roughly it spans the ages of twelve through eighteen. Even though identity has its normative crisis in adolescence, it is in reality a process which begins with the first true meeting of mother and baby, and it only ends with the waning of a person's power of mutual affirmation. In many ways the identity crisis is determined by what went on before adolescence, and it will determine much that comes afterward. The crisis of identity results from the new possibility which adolescents have by virtue of a new mental maturity. They can wonder about what others think of them; they can conceive of families and religion and societies other than their own; they can theorize about what they think and see. At this stage young people are striving to integrate all of their new thoughts and feelings into a harmonious whole.

The identity sought is both personal and social. It is personal in the sense that adolescents seek to free themselves from parents and to bring together everything they know of themselves from the past into a view of who they now are and what they might be. It is social in the sense that Crane Brinton means when he writes: "All people have some desire to locate themselves in a 'system,' a 'universe,' a process.'"[9]

It is the latter which Erikson calls the ideological component of the identity crisis. By "ideological component" he refers to "a system of ideals which societies present to the young in explicit and implicit form."[10] It is his view that without some ideological commitment young people continue to suffer diffusion of identity.

Such a step is possible because of what Erikson calls the virtue of *fidelity*. Fidelity is the capacity to perceive and abide by the values of a particular living system. In a conversation with Richard Evans, Erikson said: "We have almost an instinct for fidelity—meaning that when you reach a certain age you can and must learn to be faithful to some ideological world view."[11]

The "ideologically undernourished" young people of our land

are looking for a framework within which and for which to live. Having found such a system they are prepared to join forces with it and to put great energy at its disposal—to yield it the utmost fidelity.

The church is probably guilty of what Erikson has spoken of as "a certain abrogation of responsibility . . . in providing those forceful ideals which must antecede identity formation in the next generation."[12] Bearing as we do a powerful source of "ideological" commitment, we ought to view the teenage years as a period of special readiness for presenting the call to be a servant of Christ in the Kingdom of God.

Only in adolescence and beyond is the capacity for full faith available to a person. The cognitive ability to handle religious thought in depth gives a new profundity to the issues of religion. Studies have consistently shown that adolescence is the most religiously active period in the life cycle; it is the time of most conversion experiences. Anyone who is concerned about opening the door of faith will do well to view middle and late adolescence as the "teachable moment" *par excellence.* The trend in American denominations to move confirmation and communicant classes away from childhood and early adolescence toward middle and late teen years is in part a response to understandings of youth such as we have discussed here.

### The Faith Style of Adulthood

In American society it is hardly possible for a person to grow up without being conscious, however vaguely, of the Christian world-view and values. Thus Christianity or some version of it is an option with which most youth in our culture have to reckon—either to accept or reject. Besides the normal efforts of youth to gain some freedom from their own parental and societal matrix at least two other factors now conspire to set the rising generation on edge in regard to Christianity:

1. Familiarity with the other great religious traditions of the world makes lively possibilities out of hitherto remote faith options.

2. The relativistic and naturalistic teachings of schools and colleges cause many to call into question the validity of all cultural and religious heritages.

For many the onset of adulthood finds them drifting far from the center of Christian faith. Nonetheless, many persons—though certainly not all—find themselves being drawn back to a personally reinterpreted and reconstituted version of their religious tradition. A clear example is that of Dag Hammarskjold. *Markings,* a record of his pilgrimage, is now a classic. Few, however, are aware that shortly after his "conversion" in the early 1950s he gave a statement of his faith to Edward R. Murrow for the radio program, "This I Believe."

> I now recognize and endorse unreservedly those very beliefs which were handed down to me. . . . When I finally reached that point, the beliefs in which I was once brought up and which, in fact, had given my life direction even while my intellect still challenged their validity, were recognized by me as mine in their own right and by free choice. I feel that I can endorse those convictions without any compromise with the demands of that intellectual honesty which is the very key to maturity of mind.[14]

He then goes on to explain how the ideals of his childhood were harmonized and adjusted in his mind by his study of the ethics of Albert Schweitzer and the spirituality of the great medieval mystics. The Hammarskjold statement answers in almost every particular Lloyd J. Averill's comments on adult faith:

> When, in growing maturity, we leave our parents to strike out on our own, we can never return as the children we once were, nor should we want to . . . but maturity need not alienate us permanently from our spiritual roots. It may, rather, make possible a deeper understanding and a richer significance than was ever there before.[15]

To infer that there is an automatic return to Christianity on the part of most adults in our society is to claim false comfort. It might also encourage neglect of church responsibility for those adults who continue to be estranged from the roots of their childhood faith. Our task is to actively encourage and assist the process of rediscovering, rethinking, and recommitting life to Jesus Christ. Church school teachers, friends, and pastors will do well to be alert to this often present, but seldom spoken struggle of younger and middle-aged adults both in and out of the church. With the passage of the years we will undoubtedly find that more and more persons come to adulthood without benefit of clergy, Sunday school teachers, or Christian parents. As our society tends increasingly to be happily pagan and militantly humanistic, fewer will know anything from firsthand experience of the Christian community. Whatever support the legacy of a broadly Christian upbringing may have been for church recruitment, assistance from this source likely will diminish. The need now, and increasingly in the future, will be for the church to learn ever fresh ways to communicate with good news to those who have never heard or seen lived the gospel story. In chapter 1 we read of the birth of faith in two such persons, Francoise Mallet-Jorris and B. P. Dotsenko. Such conversions are not unusual. Those in mission lands as well as those reported in the New Testament are of this type. Yet in America, for the foreseeable future, most of those whom the church will be hoping to bring to faith will have had at least minimal exposure to the Christian way. Our evangelistic desire must be that all adults, regardless of the amount of quality of early influence, will come to full Christian faith.

Maturity of years does not guarantee maturity of faith. In some grown-ups the faith style of childhood is still dominant. Some function with an institutional faith rather than a personal faith in Christ. Others, with a partial relationship, draw down the consolations of a trusting relation with God but contribute little or nothing by way of loyal service to his name. Neurotic adults will have their faith encumbered and distorted by their personal struggles. Of course none of us has the maturity or fullness of faith in Christ that God intends for us. Our hope must be that by his grace we and others will have a lively faith that is growing toward wholeness.

## Criteria of the Person in Evangelism

Of several different criteria that might be derived from the data presented so far, we submit three as of special relevance to the task of evangelism and nurture.

1. *Each person has a unique faith story.* The more one ponders case histories of faith development, the more impressed one is with the almost infinite varieties of experience persons have with God even within the same Christian tradition. Accordingly, we should concentrate diligently on knowing each person in his uniqueness instead of approaching everyone in a standardized manner.

2. *Persons have a readiness for "full" faith in adolescence and in adulthood.* The possibility of faith, even if only in a rudimentary and partial form, is present from birth onward. In the earlier stages of life it appears that faith, and with it one's conscious relationship to God, is mediated primarily by parents and religious institutions. In the later stages the relationship of faith, though not without social sources, is more discriminating, direct, and personal. Those of us concerned to open the door of faith will do well to view the first years as a time for laying the foundation on which in later years the edifice of full faith may be erected.

3. *Persons have a developing capacity for faith.* There is a faith style more or less appropriate to each stage of life. The faith of an adult differs from that of a child. As we would not expect an adult to have a child's faith style, so we would not wish to impose adult faith expectations on a child.

While a person's faith may come to a climax at some particular time of decision and commitment, that moment has been prepared by a long pre-history and will be followed by a future of growth. Evangelism and nurture must not ignore their responsibilities before or after that time.

FOR FURTHER REFLECTION

1. The realities of faith readiness and development discussed in this chapter are not foreign to the experience of any of us, though the details differ with each person. To understand that the issues here are not just academic, it is suggested that each reader retrace his/her own

faith story. Under the five stages—infancy, early childhood, childhood, youth, adulthood—write as much as you remember or know of your faith at each period. With this in hand go over it with friends; if they ask you questions you'll likely recall more information. Compare your own faith pilgrimage with the general pattern set out in the chapter. How are they alike, unlike? Your faith experiences and those of others with whom you talk can be used to flesh out what is said here about the various faith styles. The truth is no one fully understands when a specific person is ready for faith or how faith develops.

2. If you're studying this with a congregational group or class, you might assign a few people to make a report on each one of the faith styles. Encourage them to affirm, argue with, or add to the material in the text. Ask them to list specific things that your church can do for the faith of those in the stage they are reviewing.

3. One of the main findings of this chapter is that persons are ready for full faith in adolescence and adulthood. Many people feel uneasy with this conclusion. Doesn't this go against the words of Jesus about having faith as a little child? Haven't we all seen remarkable faith in young children? This is a good issue for discussion. The answer may lie in understanding what is meant by "full" faith, i.e. a centered, relational, personal act.

4. "Helping Youth Into a Life of Faith" is the title of a section in Merton Strommen's *Five Cries of Youth*.[16] While you might want to read this, before doing so make your own set of recommendations on the same topic. What can a parent do to help? A church? A youth group?

5. Here are two case studies with a few comments. They may help you relate the ideas of this chapter to the work of evangelism. What would be your evangelistic approach to such persons?

a. Albert is the product of a broken home. His parents were divorced soon after his birth. His mother worked and left him in the care of a part-time maid. At other times he lived with an unsympathetic aunt, a chronic alcoholic. Albert never really belonged to any "gang." While in school he had few boyhood friends. He dropped out of high school after two years and found low-paid employment. He was married to a quiet, shy girl at the age of twenty-two. Through her efforts Albert is now enrolled in a young adult church school class. He is violently critical and "against the world" at times; at other times he is moody, depressed and uncommunicative.

Albert has come to young adulthood with a deficit of basic trust. His disposition suggests that not only faith in other people but faith in God may be hard won. However, in Erikson's view (which is not as pessimistic as Freud's), an Albert-type person has the possibility of overcoming his deficiency. In this case, Albert's wife and church group have the possibility of making deposits against his deficit of basic trust so that his confidence in others, in the world, and hopefully in God will be encouraged.

b. Earl, a boy of sixteen, has no real musical talent but he has identified with a long-haired group of rock-and-roll singers. He refuses to study and spends most of his time adjusting or practicing on his guitar. Several times in recent weeks he has been absent from high school class in order to accompany his musical group to other cities. He refuses to discuss the matter of his future with either of his parents. While Earl has not attended church or Sunday school for over two years, he still retains a liking for Wilson Young, a former teacher of the class.

Earl has made an identity plunge. By its nature it is not likely to prove ultimately satisfying. The church should reflect on the possibility suggested by Erikson's point-of-view—that Earl is seeking an all-embracing cause or system of meaning within which to discover his own identity and for which to live. Though having only a tenuous contact with him, the church should do all it possibly can to demonstrate in a viable and challenging way the Christian faith and life.

6. Frederick Sontag, the theologian-philosopher, reminds us "Faith may settle down on a grown man who is secular to his core with no previous experience in religion." Of what significance is this reminder as we seek to reach adults outside the church? Perhaps you'll want to review the faith stories of the Russian scientist and French author in chapter 1.

7. In chapter 1 Dave Stoner and Agnes Campbell are examples of persons who had been church members for years before they had an awakening of faith. Many suggest that in America where most people are church members, the real issue before us is how to vitalize the faith of adult church members. A look at the section on faith style of adults and the last pages of chapter 7 may give some helpful clues on how to proceed. What in your opinion are the best ways to awaken the faith of adults?

8. There is an old debate in the church between nurture and evangelism. Mainline Christians have usually come down on the side of nurture. With deprecating the importance of nurture, the necessity of conversion which flows from a decision of faith is now being stressed by some significant educators, among them John Westerhoff.

We can nurture persons into institutional religion, but not into mature Christian faith. The Christian faith by its very nature demands conversion. We do not gradually educate persons to be Christian. Of course, conversion can and indeed often has been misunderstood and overemphasized, but that does not justify our disregarding it as one necessary purpose of Christian education. . . . Conversion is therefore best understood as a radical turning from faith given (through nurture) to faith owned. Conversion is radical because it implies ownership and the corresponding transformation of our lives. It implies a turning from one style of faith to another and as such is characterized by a total reorientation in our thinking, feeling and willing.[17]

# 6 | Establishing a Faith Priority in Your Congregation

Samuel Shoemaker, Episcopal clergyman, to whose leadership the current renewal in the Church owes so much, took very seriously the call of Jesus to share faith. Of his own ministry Shoemaker wrote:

I stay near the door.
The door is the most important door in the world.
It is the door through which men walk when they find God.
Men die outside that door, as starving beggars die on cold
    nights in the dead of winter—
They live on the other side of it . . .
Go in, great saints, go all the way in.
I admire people who go way in,
But I wish they would not forget how it was before they got in.
You can go in too deeply, and stay too long,
And forget people outside the door.
Nothing else matters compared to helping them find the door
And open it, and walk in and find him.[1]

Do you believe that opening the door of faith is that important? Do you want to help your congregation do a better job of sharing Christian faith with outsiders and insiders? The church generally, and your congregation specifically, needs to make up its mind on this issue. To be effective in evangelism and education—or, for that matter in social service and action—faith must be at the top of our agenda. A faith priority for your Church? In what follows you are asked to consider the possibility.

Experience teaches that the word "faith" is often used imprecisely. By the earlier discussion of faith as a centered, relational, and personal act, you can see that we are trying to "tighten up" the definition.

1. Christian faith is a centered act—a focussing of one's personality on Jesus Christ, the Son of God (chapter 2).

2. Christian faith is a relational act—a dynamic relationship of trust in Jesus the Savior and loyalty to Jesus the Lord (chapter 3).

3. Christian faith is a personal act—a person's free choice of Christ made from alternatives (chapter 4).

When persons have this kind of faith, they become new creatures (2 Corinthians 5:17); they are reborn (John 3:7); they are converted (1 Thessolonians 1:9–10). Such faith is the solvent of prejudice and the catalyst of social action. It is the very basis of life with God and as such has been recognized in all times and places as "saving faith."

Thus, when we ask that a faith priority be considered, something quite specific is meant by faith—it is a freely chosen relationship of trust and loyalty in Jesus Christ. Now we must further refine what is meant by the term by drawing a distinction between faith, belief and religion. Then, perhaps, we will be prepared to say whether or not we think a faith priority is the urgent need of the church today.

## Faith and Religion

In a class John Westerhoff asked the group to take a sheet of paper and write on the top of one side "faith" and on the other side "religion," and then to make a brief statement of what they thought faith was and what they thought religion was. Here are some of the views expressed.

| Faith | Religion |
|---|---|
| 1. Inward and personal "me believing." | 1. Outward and corporate "we believing." |
| 2. One's reasponses to the important. | 2. The forms that one uses to respond to the important. |
| 3. Trusting and obeying. | 3. Visible embodiment of faith in beliefs, rituals, symbols, etc. |
| 4. Personal, responsive, integrative, unique. | 4. Rules and regulations, rituals and rites. |

While the two terms "faith" and "religion" are often used interchangeably (as when people speak of Christian faith, Christian religion, my faith, my religion) this simple analysis demonstrates that a distinction can and probably should be made.

⌐Faith is something more personal and inward; religion has to do with things that are more corporate and external.)Karl Barth, for example, insists that Christian faith is not Christian religion. As a part of religion he includes Christian theology, worship, forms of fellowship and church order, Christian morals, poetry and art, and all the strategies and tactics employed by the church. Former Professor of World Religions at Harvard W. C. Smith follows Barth in this distinction, though he uses the phrase "cumulative tradition" instead of "religion":

> By "faith" I mean personal faith . . . inner religious experience . . . the impingement on man of the transcendent. By "cumulative tradition" I mean . . . temples, scriptures, theological systems, dance patterns, legal and other social institutions, conventions, moral codes, myths . . . anything that can be transmitted from one generation to another and that an historian can observe.[2]

Smith goes beyond Barth, however, in helping us see that faith, though not to be equated with cumulative tradition, rises only in the midst of it.

> Each person is presented with a "cumulative tradition" and grows up among other persons to whom that tradition is meaningful. From it and them . . . he comes to a faith of his own. The tradition . . . and his fellows . . . nourish his faith and give it shape.[3]

Faith grows in a garden of religion but is not the same thing as religion.

### Faith and Belief

You will have noted that beliefs, religious statements, and theological formulations are included in what is meant by cumulative tradition or religion. In Protestantism the terms "belief" and "faith" are so closely tied that some of the historical distinctions between the two can profitably be noted.

*Kierkegaard* distinguished "objective truth" from "subjective truth," by which he meant "truth for me," a faith that achieves "contemporaneousness with Christ."
*Calvin* spoke of "saving faith" in opposition to the general believing of doctrine.
*Luther* spoke of faith concerning God and faith in God; the latter implied a personal relationship to trust.
Intellectual formulations, whether in Scriptures, creeds, or confessions, are not faith. They are the language and symbols of faith which point beyond themselves to God in Christ. This does not mean that sound doctrine is unimportant. None of the persons cited drew that conclusion. It does warn those whose goal is faith not to be satisfied with mere intellectual assent. Evangelists and educators will labor for that "more" which is trust, devotion, and obedience to that One to whom all Christian doctrine points.
Faith is not religion. Faith is not belief. Each differs from the other but as we shall see in the next chapter they are interlocking and necessary aspects of the life of any church.

**The Priority of Faith**

The argument of this chapter is not that faith is better than belief or religion—only that it is prior to them.
It is prior in the same sense that
—a door must be passed through as one enters a house
—a foundation must be laid before a building can be erected
—a first step must be taken to begin a journey
—a root must be healthy and well established for a tree to grow and bear fruit
—a prerequisite course must be passed to gain admission to an advanced course.
As each of these is a means to an end, so is faith. It is the door, foundation, first step, root, prerequisite for the Christian life. It is in this quite literal sense that faith may be said to have priority.
Faith is first. People must come through the door of faith if they are to be a part of the household of faith, partake of the bread of life, and share in the work of God's family. Faith in Christ is the channel that opens our lives to all God would bestow on us. Faith is the relationship by means of which we are motivated to enter a

working partnership with Christ in the Church and the world. The point can be put in a set of propositions. Think about them, discuss them, debate them, correct them, add to them.

✓ 1. WITHOUT FAITH IN CHRIST GOD'S BENEFITS AND GIFTS WILL NOT BECOME PART OF A PERSON'S LIFE.

Faith is the precondition for our receiving the other graces God desires to give:

| | |
|---|---|
| Forgiveness of sins (Acts 10:43) | Peace (Romans 5:1) |
| Adoption (John 1:12; Romans 8:15b–16) | Victory (1 John 5:4–5) |
| Justification (Romans 3:21–26; Romans 10:10) | Salvation (Ephesians 2:8–9; Acts 16:31) |
| Understanding (Hebrews 11:3) | Life (John 20:31) |
| Joy (Philippians 1:25) | |

✓ 2. WITHOUT FAITH IN CHRIST PERSONS ARE NOT MOTIVATED TO BECOME CO-WORKERS WITH GOD IN CHURCH AND WORLD.

Only those who know and trust the Lord answer the call to be his partners in pastoral care, social service, parenthood, social and political action, Christian education, evangelism, etc. Through the relationship of faith Christians open themselves to the energy of God that powers the church. Through faith they are inspired to give extravagantly of their physical, emotional, intellectual, and material resources. (Acts 9:1–30; Galatians 2:20; 2 Corinthians 8:1–5; John 15:1–11)

✓ 3. WITHOUT FAITH IN CHRIST THERE WILL BE NO CHRISTIAN COMMUNITY.

Persons gather in congregations, denominations, and other Christian groups because of "one faith" centered in "one Lord"

(Ephesians 4:5). From the beginning a shared faith has been the cohesive force which has brought and held Christians together (Acts 2:44; 4:32). It continues to be the magnet which unifies Christians across denominational and confessional lines.

## Faith Is Not Our Only Business

In calling the church to a faith priority it would be easy to engage in overkill. This would be disastrous. Faith may be the Alpha, but is not the Rho, Delta, Upsilon, or Omega of the Christian life.

- FAITH WITHOUT SOUND DOCTRINE IS UNDISCIPLINED, OFTEN UNINTELLIGIBLE.
- FAITH WITHOUT WORKS OF LOVE AND JUSTICE IS "NOTHING BUT DEAD."
- FAITH WITHOUT NURTURE AND INSTRUCTION REMAINS IMMATURE.
- FAITH WITHOUT ORGANIZATION HAS NO INSTRUMENT OF EXPRESSION.

As essential as a faith priority is for our day, it is possible for it to be interpreted perversely and narrowly. Unfortunately there are always those ready to latch onto a falsely spiritual notion of the church; they are anti-education, anti-social action, anti-theology, anti-institution. A faith priority rightly understood will not give aid and comfort to these who undermine the church's mission.

But isn't a faith priority a retreat from the great public and social issues of the day in favor of an individualistic and privatized version of Christianity? Millions are dying of starvation and suffering injustice. The three "Es"—energy, ecology, economy—threaten global disaster. Racism, sexism, ageism stunt the life possibilities of the race. Doesn't a faith priority suggest a cop-out on these signals of doom? It can. It need not, however, if we are wise enough to hold a broad-gauged understanding of God's work in the world.

The following chart, a modification of Loren Mead's matrix of evangelism, shows some of the ways God works in the world through his church.[4]

## HOW GOD WORKS IN THE WORLD THROUGH HIS PEOPLE

### Witness of Personal Evangelism

Most of the formal evangelism programs of denominations and of local congregations. Lay witness movements, the prayer group movement, the healing ministry movement . . . Leighton Ford, Billy Graham.

### Witness of Laity in Vocation

Secular saints of our time (like) Hammarskjold . . . We can recognize the private power of his faith . . . and we can know of his work. But there are others, mostly unknown, who live an intense faith, and who pour out their lives in mute servant style wherever they happen to be.

### Witness of Social Service

Church orphanage and adoption agencies, homes for senior citizens, religious centers for treatment of alcoholics, chaplaincies, and similar movements, institutions or leaders.

### Witness of Social and Political Action

Movement(s) concerned with national issues of war and peace, of economic justice and housing . . . The social witness of William Temple and Reinhold Neibuhr . . . denominational funds for community development and . . . power to the powerless, etc.

Each of these ways of witnessing is a legitimate expression of God's work in the world through his people. Moreover, denial of the validity of one or more of these dimensions of mission would be a negation of some aspect of our biblical heritage and Christian tradition. Any Christian congregation or denomination that desires to give a faithful and full witness must be open to God working through it in each of these ways. The church needs a fresh recognition that we who serve God in diverse ways are on one team—Christians with specialized callings and gifts. This ought to be honored as God's way of reaching out to humankind, meeting not one but the full range of our needs as persons. God's activity in the world is far more varied than our experience within one congregation or denomination tells us. But—and this is the point here—as we have visualized the breadth and scope of God's work, we have minimized, in the recent past, the work of evangelism, i.e., seeking to bring persons to faith in Christ.

A Presbyterian group, after speaking of the mission of God's church in the world as struggling for justice, relieving pain, healing hurt, and working to end war, described God's faith-work in these terms:

God is at work leading all people to know him. He has made human beings so they cannot be satisfied even with justice, compassion and peace on earth. They are hungry for God himself. He is grieved when many remain ignorant of his love. God is at work where men and women are concerned to share faith with their neighbors in word and life. He sends us to tell the good news to all humankind.[5]

This is not the only work of the church, but if the argument of this chapter is correct, it is the *first* work.

To further clarify for those who feel uneasy on this point, persons are co-workers with God in social service, social and political action, and in the realm of vocation because they have first come through the door of faith. So far as my experience goes, Martin Marty's statement is correct: "Most of the creative participants in Christian action are people shaped by conservative and evangelistic religion."[6] An emphasis on faith and evangelism, which is one part of God's mission, is not going to satisfy the claimant demands on it for relevant social action. Yet I venture to predict that some persons brought to a developing relationship of faith in Christ in one of our congregations will be answering, in decades to come, the call to serve God in his total mission in the world. Or, to put this negatively, if persons don't come first to personal faith, they will never be working—consciously, at least—with God in any activity whether in church or society.

**Only the Church Is in This Business**

No other organization on planet earth really thinks sharing Christian faith is an important, urgent, and worthwhile undertaking. A Houston pastor spoke to this issue in a recent sermon:

Others in our society can provide more professional entertainment and counseling services. The government has more money to spend in working with disadvantaged. But where are people to find a confidence that life is worth living when all they can see or feel around them is hopelessness and pain? Where can people go to experience their personal worth as loved children of God in a society becoming increasingly massive and mechanized? . . . We are a people who know what it is to be loved and forgiven better than we deserve. We have experienced a new hope arising within us when we were crumbled in the ashes of despair. By the grace of Almighty God, faith has been given to us. Now it is ours to share.[7]

Again, we are not arguing that Christian faith is our *only* business but that, if we do not make it our business, nobody else will!

### A Faith Priority in Your Church?

Wishing will not make it so! A faith priority will be set only by policy decisions of church leaders at all levels. Some may argue that we now have—always have had—a faith priority. I doubt that. Issues of *religion,* such as restructuring of organizations and refurbishing of personnel policies, along with issues of *belief,* such as reformulating creeds and refining mission statements, seem to be getting the lion's share of time, energy, and money. Dollar for dollar, hour for hour, I suspect faith issues are now coming in second or third best in our congregations and denominations. You and I can change that if we think it is right and important.

### A Faith Priority in Your Life?

It is not enough that the church in general or your congregation in particular have a faith priority. Each of us must be concerned for ourselves and others that we have and are growing in Christian faith.

All our study to this point of the meaning of faith, all future discussions of mobilizing congregations for witness will be to no avail unless we really care whether persons believe in Jesus Christ as Lord and Savior.

At the Evanston Assembly, D. T. Niles asked a vast congregation of church men and women: "Can you mention the names of people, two or three perhaps, who are to you a real sorrow because they are not Christians? They are good people, they are your friends, but always when you think of them there is a pain in your soul because they do not serve Jesus Christ. Are there such people in your life? If not you are not an evangelist." With Sam Shoemaker, will you "stay near the door" so that persons may "open it, and walk in and find Him"?

**FOR FURTHER REFLECTION**

1. State in your own words what Christian faith is. Why does the author stress getting a good clear definition of faith?

2. Suppose you were asked to make a presentation to your church board or to the congregation at worship on "why our Church ought to adopt a faith priority." Draft a brief outline of the speech you would make.

3. As much as the author stresses faith, he seems to fear that the faith priority idea can be misused. Are his worries justified? What can be done to minimize this risk?

4. The distinctions of faith, belief, and religion are not found in the Bible. Certain theologians have found them useful, however. Do they give you insight into your life, your congregation? Does their use help you focus on what faith is?

5. There are some large claims for faith in this chapter. How does faith open one to the benefits of God such as forgiveness, peace, joy, salvation? How does a faith relationship motivate persons to work with Christ in the church and the world? How does a common faith in Christ serve as a magnet drawing Christians of diverse persuasions together?

6. In the chart on "How God Works in the World," the section on "The Witness of Social and Political Action" may seem strange to some, to others controversial. What is clear is that in America some Christians have felt that God was calling them to change the existing social arrangement—the revolutionary war, abolition movement, right of labor to organize, women's suffrage, civil rights movement, etc. Also, many missionaries, such as those in India who sought to change the caste system, have been among those who felt God's work included social change. Do you believe God cares about our social organizations? That he wants them improved or changed?

7. Do you agree with the author's view that, unless persons come first to personal faith, they will not be working with God—consciously at least—in any activity whether in church or society?

8. Think over the D. T. Niles quotation. Are you prepared to accept the criticism and challenge implied in it?

9. After all is said and done, do you plan to work for a faith priority in your life, in your church? How?

# 7 | Renewing the Faith Life of Your Congregation

In the United States the normative religious structure is the congregation.* 72,000,000 persons belong to approximately 300, 000 congregations in America. The average size is 240 members. These congregations are in every section of the country. They include people of every social class and race. They are composed of children, parents, and grandparents. They touch life at birth, puberty, and adulthood. When we make our exit from life they provide warm personal support coupled with life sustaining symbols of the Christian faith. Week by week people come together in them for worship. In these congregations the natural forces of human interaction are at work. In their fellowship faith is born and sustained.

Loren Mead of the Episcopal Church's Project Test Pattern has done much to promote a recovery of confidence among some of us in congregations. In a taped conversation he speaks

---

*Note: While we are using the term "congregation" in order to emphasize the usual institutional expression of the church, it should be pointed out that Christian community effectively takes many forms—monasteries, communes, house churches, adult Sunday School classes, as well as the various fellowships which exist for students, business persons, etc. The essential characteristics required of such communities have been described by C. Ellis Nelson in the following way:

"What a community of believers must have is face-to-face personal relations of enough permanence for the group to worship, work, and study together under a common commitment to the God of the Bible."

"The local congregation should be of such size and so organized that the communal reality can most readily develop and be experienced by its members." (From *Where Faith Begins*, John Knox Press, 1967, p. 34, p. 99. See sections on "Communal Reality" and "The Gathered Christians," pp. 97–102.)

movingly of some of the functions of the parish. His view is that congregations do three things which no other institution does so well.

1. They keep us in close touch with Scripture.
2. They keep us in close touch with people.
3. They keep us in close touch with God.[1]

The time has come to stop undervaluing and underutilizing our congregations in the work of faith transmission.

Where congregations with faith in Christ exist, our view is that they are the most powerful instruments available to the church for evangelism and nurture. The center of all persons' faith and the focus of their life's loyalties will be determined in large measure by the congregation in which they participate. Each congregation is a bearer of a religious tradition which is the product of the faith of men and women in the past, and potentially an avenue for the faith of men and women in the present.

Having made these large claims, however, they need to be qualified. Even though we love and affirm our churches, we know they can be improved and made more productive. We rejoice in the good they do, but rightly we sense they can be better. The key question to ask and answer is: How can our congregation more effectively awaken or call forth full Christian faith as a freely chosen relationship of trust and loyalty centered in the Father, Son, and Holy Spirit?

## The Interlocking System of Faith, Belief, and Religion

One way to approach this issue is suggested by the distinction drawn in chapter six between faith, belief, and religion.

Life in a congregation can be described as an interlocking relationship of these three.[2]

1. Faith has to do with deep convictions and core values arising from encountering and experiencing the gospel, life, and God.

2. Belief has to do with the ways we think and talk about our deep faith convictions; theological interpretations, creeds, statements of purpose and goals, and conversations about our faith are examples of belief.

3. Religion refers to what we do and ways we behave when we are gathered as the church and when we are scattered in the world. Church programs of stewardship, nurture, and evangelism; worship and sacraments; ways we treat other persons; social service rendered; political actions taken—these are a few examples of what is meant by religion.

If the faith, belief, and religion of a congregation are strong and if they are integrally related, there is maximum possibility that persons coming to contact with the life of the church will be encouraged to affirm its core values as their own faith. However, if a congregation is severely incapacitated at one or more of these levels, if its beliefs don't carry over into consistent behaviors, if its strong convictions are uninstructed by its theological tradition, if its beliefs and behaviors are not motivated by its faith, etc., then the possibility of its successfully communicating the Christian faith is lessened.

While faith, belief, and religion may be distinguished for purposes of analysis, they are tied together in the life of a church organization. Weakness at any of these three levels, or a lack of consistency between them, will impair the functioning of a congregation or denomination. Vital churches are those which again and again touch base with their faith, reformulate their statements of belief and purpose, and engage in new actions and behaviors which are congruent with their faith and belief. The "tree" diagram will assist our understanding of these relationships.

An obvious conclusion from this illustration is that a congregation, like a tree, cannot function adequately in any aspect of its life unless each level is healthy.

## Analyzing Your Own Congregation

In every congregation there are persons who wish that their church could do a better job of assisting individuals toward faith. Their concern reaches outside to non-members and inside to children and youth, as well as adult inactives. When denominational leaders respond to churches seeking such help, they usually offer a new program method with, perhaps, some new content.

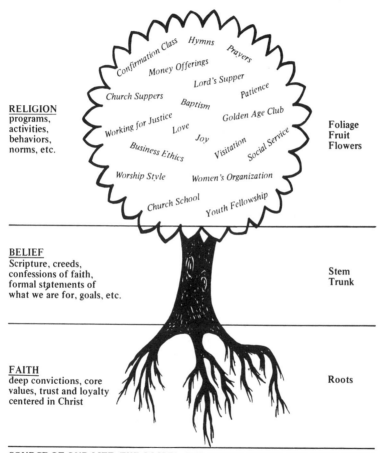

**RELIGION**
programs,
activities,
behaviors,
norms, etc.

Confirmation Class Hymns Prayers
Money Offerings
Lord's Supper
Church Suppers Patience
Baptism
Working for Justice Golden Age Club
Love
Joy
Business Ethics Visitation Social Service
Worship Style Women's Organization
Church School Youth Fellowship

Foliage
Fruit
Flowers

**BELIEF**
Scripture, creeds,
confessions of faith,
formal statements of
what we are for, goals, etc.

Stem
Trunk

**FAITH**
deep convictions, core
values, trust and loyalty
centered in Christ

Roots

SOURCE OF OUR LIFE=THE GOSPEL, THE LIVING CHRIST, THE HOLY SPIRIT

OPENING THE DOOR OF FAITH

The general assumption is that a change at the level of religion (method) will bring the needed transformation. Of course, a new method of discovery learning or visitation evangelism may be just what is needed. But, on the other hand, if the faith and belief levels are not firmly in place, the resulting lack of motivation or clarity of purpose may be too shaky a foundation upon which to build any evangelism program successfully.

Before decisions can be made about what to do to improve any aspect of the life of a congregation there must be some clear-headed insight into the situation of the particular church. Each congregation is unique; each has its own special blend of members; in each the mix of faith, belief, and religion varies. Those, then, who really want to do something about improving their congregation's capacity for opening the door of faith must know something about the inner dynamics of their fellowship. Here is a way to get an approximate view of a congregation's faith, belief, religion. Make copies of the following chart; fill it in yourself. Ask friends in your church to do the same.

| | True | | | | | | | | | False |
|---|---|---|---|---|---|---|---|---|---|---|
| RELIGION | 1 | 2 | 3 | 4 | 5 | 6 | 7 | 8 | 9 | 10 |

Our congregation has programs, services, activities that adequately communicate our faith and beliefs.

| | True | | | | | | | | | False |
|---|---|---|---|---|---|---|---|---|---|---|
| BELIEF | 1 | 2 | 3 | 4 | 5 | 6 | 7 | 8 | 9 | 10 |

Our congregation really knows what it believes and what it is for.

| | True | | | | | | | | | False |
|---|---|---|---|---|---|---|---|---|---|---|
| FAITH | 1 | 2 | 3 | 4 | 5 | 6 | 7 | 8 | 9 | 10 |

Our congregation is filled with people of deep Christian convictions and strong faith in Christ.

(Circle the number on each scale above that you believe best describes your congregation).

When you have several charts in hand, compare them and derive an average score for each.

Now suppose the composite RELIGION score is 8, the BELIEF score is 5, and the FAITH score is 3. What you have in hand is a guess about these aspects of the life of your church. In this example, those responding see their church as being stronger at the FAITH level and weaker at the RELIGION level. To check your findings there are two other things you might do: 1. Make a list of the main organizations in your church—women, youth, boards, classes. Ask members of those groups to fill in a chart on their group. (Be sure they respond in terms of their group and not the whole church). Compile the data group by group. Finally, total all the charts and compare with your preliminary judgment about the whole congregation. 2. With this data in hand, check it another way. Become a participant observer. For a given period of time (say three weeks) pay very close attention to the life of your congregation in regard to its FAITH, BELIEF, and RELIGION. Read the newsletter with this in mind, watch for evidences of each at worship services, youth programs, board meetings, small group gatherings, etc. Select, and interview a variety of members—young, old; active, inactive; officers, non-officers; men, women; newcomers, oldtimers; etc. Throughout the process keep a notebook. Afterward, review the data recorded. Does it tend to confirm or deny your original hunches about your church's FAITH, BELIEF, and RELIGION? Review your original thoughts in light of your new findings.

The process we have been describing is not going to give an absolutely true picture of your church, but it is better than the offhand impressions of only a few people. With this data you now have some notion of where the strengths and weaknesses are perceived in your congregation's faith, belief, and religion. You know that some groups have more of one than the other.

The next step is to look for and utilize the people-resources in your church. The hopeful thing about most of our congregations is that there are strengths at each level, i.e., there are people who obviously are strong in faith, or belief, or religion—or all three. Such persons need to be clearly identified, their strengths affirmed and cultivated. Talk to them about your concern. Enlist their aid.

**Motivation, Message and Method?**

In the work of evangelism, as well as education, there are three basic components. Each is related to one of the three levels; an examination of them will further clarify the issue before us:

1. *Motivation* (Faith)

The motivation for evangelism and nurture springs up in persons who energized by deep faith convictions.

2. *Message or Content* (Belief)

The message of faith as communicated in evangelism and nurture is clarified by those who have thought through with others their deep faith experience and commitments in the light of Scripture and their theological tradition.

3. *Method* (Religion)

Methods are developed by those highly motivated persons who have a message to share; methods must be adequate to the task and appropriate to the end sought, namely faith in Christ as a centered, relational, and personal act.

Some congregations possess the programs and skills to pass on the faith, but lack clarity in regard to the message or may discover lack of interest or concern in so doing. Others are highly motivated, but garble and confuse the message, or don't organize in ways that give maximum reach to the good news they themselves feel and wish to share. Again it should be plain that each aspect—motivation, message and method—must be relatively strong and integrally related if an adequate job of communicating the faith is to be carried out.

Some group in your church, preferably one appointed by the official board, will need to think, plan, map strategy, and put in hours of hard work to bring forth the needed changes. If the deficit in evangelism is seen to be at the religion or method level, then a search for, or development of a suitable program is necessary. An abundance of resources is available to congregations. (See the resource guide provided by your denomination.) If the deficit is at the belief level, there are several approaches:

1. The most obvious is to begin some formal study of the beliefs of your own denomination or a book of the Bible such as Romans.

2. Another approach is to undertake an effort in church school classes or the whole church to write statements of what you believe.

3. In terms of moving from beliefs to behavior, it might be important for your church to undertake an effort to write goals or purposes based on what the group perceives to be its most cherished convictions and beliefs. These could then be translated into objectives to be implemented in programs.

## Renewing the Convictional Base

We now turn to a discussion of the faith level—the issue around which this book is written. Our hypothesis is that the main cause of the current ineffectiveness in our churches, whether in nurture or evangelism or social action, is related to an erosion of faith. Renewal at that level is necessary if we are to have dynamic congregations which transmit faith as a personal, centered, and relational act. Let's now discuss this point and suggest a few things to do about it.

The problem in American mainline churches at the present time is not primarily at the level of religion—we are masters at methods of communication and developing and implementing programs and campaigns; once we are motivated, ways and means will be found. Nor is the chief difficulty at the level of belief—the message we communicate. However, a general biblical illiteracy and theological ignorance in our churches does indicate the need for large efforts at this level. Nonetheless, the level of our largest deficit is at the convictional base, the motivational source which underlies both message and method.

George E. Sweazey, Moderator in 1969 of the United Presbyterian Church, spoke of this phenomena: "The real reason for the lack of evangelism in our church is the loss of religious vividness. From that comes also the loss of membership, and of benevolence giving."[3]

In the Presbyterian Church U.S., the General Assembly's Council on Evangelism held a series of feedback events in 1973 to ascertain the feelings and opinions of members about evangelism. The problem as reflected in the sessions was lack of commitment (faith), lack of comprehension (belief), lack of know-how (religion)—in that order. Of lack of commitment the report said:

The most frequently used term was *apathy*.

Other characteristic expressions used under this head were "lack of concern," "lack of love," "complacency," "laziness," "a failure to practice what we preach," etc.

There was felt to be a lack of leadership commitment at all levels, with particular emphasis on local pastors and sessions, but also a lack of commitment on the part of the congregation as a whole.

In a 1971 speech to the Denver meeting of the Consultation on Church Union, Peter Berger, Lutheran pastor and sociologist of religion, fussed at mainline Protestant churches and called them to a recovery of authority. His accusation was that too many of us are scurrying about searching for some cultural or counter-cultural god with which to identify. He spoke specifically about those who make "modern man" and "modern consciousness" into golden calves; he decried those who were falling all over themselves to be relevant. His was a prophetic warning against a too-easy accomodation with any social faith.

In Berger's opinion, recovery of confident authority must come from within the Christian tradition. What does the church have to recover? In his view it is the one story of God's dealing with the human family:

. . . The story that spans the Exodus and Easter morning. When all is said and done, the Christian community consists of those people who keep on telling this story to each other, and some of those people climb up on soap boxes of some kind to tell the story to others.[4]

This story finds its center in Jesus Christ through whom the one living God is known. The mere telling of this gospel story has proven sufficient to turn men from idols to the living God. In it is embedded our world view and from it we derive our basic values. In his view the church, having lost significant contact with the source of its life, has lost as a result its sense of identity, confidence, and strength of purpose. Only at the point where the church gets firmly in touch with its own gospel does Berger anticipate a shift from timid dialogue to proclamation.

Christian faith, as we have seen, is rooted and grounded in the gospel of God. It is activated by the grace of our Lord Jesus Christ. In this soil alone faith flourishes and grows to maturity. In a discussion of the faith crisis hypothesis, two pastors offered wise comments that hold us to this center:

We should begin by speaking of God's faith in us instead of our lack of faith in God—then we would have some inspiration to lift us from our lethargy. "Faith" in our theology is a response to what God has done for us in Jesus Christ. I am naïve enough to believe that the truth of Jesus Christ will lift the hulk of us mired in sand and set us afloat again.

To talk most about our crisis of faith instead of Christ will prove counter-productive. We need a fresh reminder of the grace of God that is bigger than whatever we do or don't do—a recovery of the promises of God, which will give us again an understanding of ourselves as the people of God able to live through this and other crises with courage and vision.

Each of these ministers, along with Peter Berger, is pressing us to the heart of the matter. The experience of faith springs from the God and Father of Jesus Christ. He is the source of our life, the author and finisher of our faith. Without him persons may have "religious" experience but not Christian faith.

## Technologies of Transmission

This is a risky but necessary point.

In the old days revivals, prayer meetings, and weeks of spiritual enrichment were means used to stir the faith convictions of congregations. For most, these have fallen out of use. There are, however, new approaches which can be adapted to the many styles of denominational tradition and congregational life. They are not magic, not sure-fire; but they are ways that have sparked congregational renewal at the faith level.

Organizations such as Faith at Work, Institute of Church Renewal, Council of Lay Life and Work of the United Church of Christ, and the Evangelism divisions of the two Presbyterian denominations have many practical techniques for faith awakening. From reading some of their materials, here are a few suggestions for you and your church:

1. Take part in weekend experiences—retreats, faith explorations, lay renewal gatherings.
2. Do private reading and reflection on a whole book of the Bible—Genesis, Mark Acts, Romans.
3. Re-examine, then recommit yourself to the various vows you have made, e.g. marriage, baptism, confirmation, ordination.
4. Participate in a small group of concerned persons who through prayer and discussion are dealing the issues of daily work, world hunger, national policies, etc.
5. Worship regularly, reflecting with others on its practical implications.
6. Explore the meaning for yourself and your congregation of some official statement of faith. Write out your own expression of what faith means to you.
7. Listen to and reflect with others upon sermons which deal with the gospel and other deep issues of faith.
8. Clarify anew your own deepest values and faith commitments.
9. Dig again with others into the Scripture searching for what it says about your life, responsibility for others, etc.
10. Reflect afresh on your own faith story/spiritual journey.

Working at the faith level is not without its risks. Having some "feeling" or "experience" can become a substitute for knowing Christ. Participating in some of the religious activities of faith awakening (as those above) can become as important to some as the object of faith. It is invariably true that faith needs to be disciplined by belief and religion, even when it is derived from a genuine encounter with the gospel.

1. Belief as expressed in Scripture, church history, and contemporary statements of faith and purpose needs to be used to instruct, clarify, and perhaps modify the new enthusiams that emerge.
2. Religion as expressed in the local church through worship, church school, visitation evangelism, and stewardship should be used to harness and channel new energies that arise.

**Conclusion**

It should be clear by now that the concern of this book is for opening the door of faith through evangelism and nurture. The author hopes for nothing less than a renewal of faith which will vitalize the church in its total ministry and mission. A recovery of faith, as defined in these pages, will in his view bear the all important fruits of faith celebration (worship), faith translation (social service and action), faith development (nurture), and faith awakening (evangelism) that reflect the wholeness of our calling under God.

**FOR FURTHER REFLECTION**

1. "The center of a person's faith and the focus of his life's loyalties will be determined in large measure by the congregation in which he participates." Does your experience indicate that this observation is correct? In what ways have congregations had a positive or negative effect on your faith? On that of others you know?

2. Ellis Nelson in the footnote at the beginning of this chapter speaks of the necessity of face-to-face interaction if congregations are to have their full potential for faith awakening. Does that exist in your congregation? Do we really meet people in our churches? How can more of this be fostered? In small congregations? In large ones?

3. Discuss the "tree chart." Clarify the author's intent in using it. Is it helpful in understanding what a healthy church is? Does it obscure or neglect or minimize some aspect of church life? How would you change it? Or, would you suggest a different illustration?

4. Almost thirty years ago Elton Truebrood wrote a book on the Ten Commandments in which he spoke of ours as a "cut flower civilization." Play around with that idea in relation to the "tree chart." What do you think he meant? Do you see any application to the church today?

5. Evaluate this quotation made by Michael Green of England at the Congress on World Evangelization 1974: "Once there is a burning passion to share Jesus with others inside your heart, you'll find a way of doing it all right without reading a manual on the subject."

   Can "burning passion to share Jesus" be created? What is the proper place of manuals on evangelism? Does Green draw an over-simplified distinction between motivation for evangelism and methods of evangelism?

6. Albert Outler, the Methodist theologian, gave lectures on John Wesley's evangelism in which he spoke of a single core of Christian faith. He then went on to say that no single set of words, no single

conceptual system is adequate to explain that core. In the New Testament we discover a variety of ways in which the one gospel was explained: incarnation, justification, Kingdom of God, reconciliation, forgiveness, etc. If asked, how would you explain the gospel? In evangelism we are not asked to parrot the words of others, but we do have to be able to explain in our own way just what the good news is. Practice explaining it to some of your classmates or friends. Writing down your interpretation of the single core of Christian faith will be a most instructive exercise and may equip you to share faith in such a way that another person will find new life in Christ.

7. As we saw in the chapter, Peter Berger calls for a recovery of authority. How does he propose that this be done? Can you work on this in your church? Will a recovery of authority lead to arrogance or authoritarianism on the part of Christians? How could such negative by-products be avoided?

8. Toward the end of the chapter there is a long list of proposals for renewing the life of the congregation at the faith level. Which of these would be useful in your church? Is there a committee of your governing board which could help put some of these into operation?

# 8 | Your Congregation— Its Potential for Communicating Faith

The marvelous work of organized religion is to provide the environment of active faith. . . .[1]

In recent years organized religion, especially its congregational expression has taken many verbal lumps. Indeed, local churches have liabilities that need correcting. But they also have many possibilities which need affirming. It is time to take a fresh look at the potential of congregations for communicating Christian faith.

A good way to do this is to examine the effect of "organized religion" on the faith life of three persons, Harvey Cox and two unnamed graduate students.

1. Harvey Cox, widely known for *The Secular City,* tells in his book *The Seduction of the Spirit* about his own faith story. It began in Malvern, a small Pennsylvania town. He remembers the Baptist church there with "a mixture of warmth, boredom, awe, guilt, and fascination." He tells of the experience of baptism by total immersion, participation in congregational business meetings, his desire to be a minister and some early doubts about doctrines taught by ministers he admired. With gratitude Cox writes about Malvern.

> It molded impulses and instincts that still move me every day. It aroused obsessions that still haunt me. It kindled longings I will feel until I die. Malvern was the place where, as I might once have said, and can still say in another way, "Jesus came into my heart," where the awful sense of the fathomless mystery and utter transiency of life first dawned on me, and where I discovered that in the midst of all that terror and

nothingness I was loved. What more could anyone's tribal village do for him?[2]

2. *Student A:*

   Organized religion has played an essential role in my faith life. It has provided in liturgical services and religious instruction the teaching and encouragement to grow in my personal relationship with God. In the religious community of which I am a member, the instruction and encouragement have continued intensely. As a result of the maturing of my faith which organized religion has fostered, my faith has achieved a certain independence of that organized religion. In prayer, reflection, and ministry I have come to an awareness of the limiting and constricting attitudes fostered by organized religion, as well as to an appreciation of the resources which organized religion provides.

3. *Student B:*

   My relationship with my particular faith community in many very important ways sustains my faith. It is an important thing for me to know that the path I have chosen has been chartered by many who have gone before. This strengthens the courage of my own religious convictions and gives me a sense of belonging to a community concern that has proven worthwhile.

   But belonging to a community of faith provides more than a heritage, a historical assurance that what I believe is worthwhile. Belonging to a covenant people gives me an opportunity to share in acts of communion with fellow believers and worship and praise of the One I believe to be the ultimate source of meaning. Without this corporate experience faith would lose some of its essence.

**The Medium and the Message**

For most people the "medium" of congregational life is the "message." The total communal life of a particular church—its members, budget, service projects, worship, women's circles, nursery attendants, church school—is a vast communications network.

Some romantics long for faith without ritual, God without tradition, Christ without communion, Christianity without congregation. This is a utopian dream. In 1962, at the height of the anti-congregation movement, James Gustafson wrote of the necessity of religious institutions.

> There may be virtuosos among us who individually can have a relationship to God without church committees, every member canvasses, and youth groups. There are fewer who can be related to Christ and to neighbor without hearing the Word of God and partaking of his Body and Blood. For ordinary and even extraordinary men, however, religious ethos is the mediating milieu in which and through which life with Christ and life in the world are joined.[3]

Every form of human enterprise, including the religious, exists in institutional form. Congregation may be lumbering, tortoise-like and moss-backed, yet it is in the midst of such structures that faith arises. If the consumptive religious institution of the Middle Ages could cough up persons like Francis and Luther, we certainly ought to take heart about the possible usefulness of our congregations in faith arousal and maintenance.

## Evangelism's Threefold Witness

In the 1950s the World Council of Churches introduced a tri-dimensional understanding of evangelism. Following the book of Acts, chapters 1 through 4, it sees witness (Acts 1:8) as an inseparable triad of proclamation (*kerygma*), service (*diakonia*) and community life (*koinonia*). In the earliest church the gospel and its power was made visible in the actual life of the community (Acts 2:44–47), the gospel was demonstrated in humble service (Acts 3:1–10), and the gospel was made audible through the spoken word (Acts 4:8–12). Effective evangelism includes all three dimensions and is incomplete when any one of the three is not incorporated in the life of a congregation.

A number of denominations have accepted this full-bodied understanding of evangelism in their program emphases or official statements. Here are examples of evangelism's threefold witness. They are set forth with the hope that they will stimulate a vision of what faithfulness and fulness in mission might mean in your congregation.

## THE WITNESS OF COMMUNITY LIFE

The love of Christians one for another in the fellowship of the Christian community is Evangelism. (Cf.
John 13:34–35; John 17.)

## THE EARLY CHURCH

If they see a stranger, they take him to their dwellings and
rejoice over him as over a real brother. For they do not call
themselves brethren after the flesh, but after the Spirit. . . .
And if they hear that one of them is imprisoned or oppressed on
account of the name of their Messiah, all of them care for his
necessity, and if it is possible to redeem him, they set him free.
And if anyone among them is poor and needy, and they have no
spare food, they fast two or three days in order to supply him
with the needed food. The precepts of their Messiah they observe
with great care. They live justly and soberly, as the Lord their
God commanded them. Every morning and every hour they
acknowledge and praise God for his loving-kindnesses toward
them, and for their food and drink they give thanks to him. And if
any righteous man among them passes from this world, they
rejoice and thank God.

Aristides

## EAST JAVA

Non-Christians in the villages began to notice the quality of life
lived by their Christian neighbors. Their curiosity caused them to
inquire about what made the difference between the quality of life
of a Christian and a non-Christian. Two things impressed them
most about the way Christians lived.

First, the inner serenity of the Christian regardless of the
dangers, the uncertainties and the adversities which he faced.
Especially were they impressed with the Christians' freedom
from fear of the powers which the East Javanese people believed
pervaded all of the natural world.

Second, they were impressed by the kind of lives which
Christians lived together both as families and in the larger
community. Christians respect each other, love each other, and
trust each other. For instance, the genuine fellowship in family

life among Christians impresses their non-Christian neighbors. The Christian families, including the wife, eat their meals together. In non-Christian families the wife waits until the rest of the family has eaten and only has whatever may be left for her meal. The Christian families sing hymns together and enjoy being with each other. Sharing their faith is a vital part of their life together. In non-Christian villages the land is owned by 5% of the population. In Christian villages the land is owned by 80% of the population. Making ownership of land possible for more people is a very practical way in which Christians in East Java show their love and concern for each other.

When non-Christians ask their Christian neighbors what makes the difference in their way of living, usually they are invited to observe Christian worship services and the Christian ways of expressing their faith together. If non-Christians continue to show an interest in the Christian way of life, they are referred to the pastor for more specific instructions in the meaning of faith. Usually a one year period of instruction precedes church membership.

H. Grady Allison, U.P.C.U.S.A. Unit on Evangelism

## U. S. A.

New town, new home, new church, suddenly tragic death—the bereaved widow writes her former pastor about the response of her new Christian friends:

The love of our church has just been overwhelming. So many folks have found their own distinct way of suffering with and supporting us. They literally have lifted us out of the darkness into the light and air of healing by their caring.

## THE WITNESS OF DEED

The life style of the Christian person and the Christian community in radical obedience to the Biblical mandates of the Kingdom of God in the world is Evangelism. (Cf. Matthew 5:14–16; Matthew 25:31ff.; Mark 12:29–31; Luke 4:16–21; John 20:21; Romans 12:1–2; Ephesians 3:10.)

## THE EARLY CHURCH

With us, you will find unlettered people, tradesmen and old women, who, though unable to express in words the advantages of our teaching, demonstrate by acts the value of their principles. For they do not rehearse speeches, but evidence good deeds.

Justin

Most of our brethren [during the Alexandrian plague] did not spare themselves and held together in the closest love of their neighbors. They were not afraid to visit the sick, to look after them well, to take care of them for Christ's sake and to die joyfully with them. . . . Many of them lost their own lives after restoring others to health, thus taking their death upon themselves. . . . In this way some of the noblest of our brethren died—some presbyters, deacons and highly-esteemed lay people. But the heathen did exactly the opposite. They cast out any people who began to be too ill, and deserted those dearest.

Bishop Dionysius

## THAILAND

Work in the Christian hospitals of Thailand consists mainly of ministering to the spiritual needs of the patients and their families while caring for the medical needs of the patients.

Archorn (Rev.) Paiboon is the chaplain at McCormick Hospital in Chiang Mai. His program of work reaches out far beyond those who are patients in the hospital. He has organized 21 prayer groups among the hospital employees. These groups meet daily for 15 minutes at times which are convenient for them. As the result of these prayer groups an evangelism team was organized by the employees of McCormick Hospital. They wanted to go out into one of the nearby villages and start a church.

After surveying the possibilities in eight nearby villages, they selected Lotus Swamp Village for the site of their labors. Using a land rover provided by the hospital, a group of five or six employees went out every weekend, visited with the people and conducted worship services in one of the homes. The work was difficult but they persevered. Last July they organized a church with 32 newly baptized converts from Buddhism. Since then 26 more have been baptized and they have a class of 20 more persons who have confessed faith in Christ and are receiving instruction in preparation for baptism.

The work of these lay people from McCormick Hospital is evangelism in its truest sense. They are concerned about the total person and about the life of the village as well. Lotus Swamp Village is very poor. In fact last year the villagers had to sell six girls from their village into prostitution in Bangkok to get money to buy the seed to plant their rice crops. The workers from McCormick Hospital obtained money this year from the Church of Christ in Thailand's Rural Life Division and lent it to the villagers to buy seed to plant rice to prevent a re-occurance of what happened last year.

In an effort to improve the economic conditions of Lotus Swamp Village these workers plan to buy 100 acres of land and sell it to the villagers at relatively low interest rates. The villagers will pay for the land out of the proceeds from the crops which they raise on the land. Archorn Paiboon, who is directing this project, figures the villagers can repay the cost of the land within five years. Then his group will use the money again for a similar project in another village. They also plan to purchase a swamp which they will make into a fish pond which will provide enough fish to supply the whole village. This plan has been approved by the Rural Life Division of the C.C.T. and will be implemented as soon as the McCormick Hospital workers can raise the $4,000.00 which they need to finance the project.

H. Grady Allison, U.P.C.U.S.A. Unit on Evangelism

## U. S. A.

The untouched are those who claim to have never had any vital religious experience. They are unchurched and usually secular to the core. The points of contact are their love for the world and compassion for persons. When they see Christian congregations organized to implement this love and compassion, they become interested.

Ed S. is a good example. He only knew the church from the outside. To him it was a place for weak, superstitious persons who need a crutch. He could stand alone, "make his own way without the hymn singing and tear jerking," his re-thinking began when he learned about the Clergy Review Board operating in Des Moines. This ecumenical task force was formed to assist young men encountering difficulties getting a fair hearing from local draft boards. Standard procedure was to interview the candidate, reach a consensus about the validity of the claim, then to communicate this consensus to the draft board. None of the sixty men interviewed were drafted; one was a personal friend of Ed's. Consequently, Ed became interested in the church and for him the evangelistic wheels were set in motion. Today, one of his gifts is the writing of contemporary liturgy.

. . . We are in a period of history when social action is winning people . . . to the Christian faith and to the institutional church. If local churches strategize to let a steady application of the Christian gospel communicate their Biblical faith, many persons will be born anew. There are several in every hamlet like the woman who testifies: "I never had time for the church until two years ago. To me it was a gathering of hypocrites trying to save their own souls. This description still fits but it is not the whole truth. I've been reading and thinking and watching. With all its imperfections, I have been forced to admit that the church has produced the people who tried to do something about the war in Vietnam, about the lies our government was telling us, about third-world hunger and poverty, and every other major threat to civilization. When other humanitarian folk give up, the church keeps plugging away. The root problem I now know is a matter of spirit. And the Christ spirit is the most nourishing I know."

Chester L. Guinn, United Methodist, Perry, Iowa

## THE WITNESS OF WORD

The proclamation of the Kingdom of God is Evangelism. (Cf. Matthew 28:19–20; Mark 1:14–15; Luke 24:45–47; John 20:21; Romans 10:14–17; John 14:5.)

[Sometime] ago I was at a meeting of an evangelism task group in New York State. One of the ministers there had developed what seemed to be a very effective style of ministry in getting certain things done in the community. He could organize task groups to work on projects. He could get people to study issues about which sincere Christians in any community ought to be concerned. He could motivate constructive action for work on situations which needed to be changed. He had a successful record of being able to raise the social consciousness of Christians regarding matters which needed their attention.

But by his own admission, he felt completely inept in the matter of sharing his faith in a meaningful way with another person who wanted to hear it, and who would be open to receive.

He simply did not know how to go about articulating the good news of God's grace revealed in Christ. He was a well educated, articulate person. Ordinarily, expressing ideas verbally was not something which gave him a problem. But when it came to sharing his faith in Christ with somebody else, it did. In the past fourteen months I have travelled over most of this nation and have talked with more people than I can remember. The one thing which has impressed me as much as anything else is simply this. *That pastor in New York State about whom I was speaking has a lot of company.* His problem is not all unique with him. Too many people in the United Presbyterian Church, both ministers and lay people, lack the ability to articulate the gospel, as reformed theology interprets it, to people who are open to receiving it.

H. Grady Allison, U.P.C.U.S.A. Unit on Evangelism

The Christian life which supposedly makes a witness without uttering a word is often reduced to inanities. Christians don't give off a special neon glow which other people can detect.

Robert Spike,
slain social activist and
minister of the gospel

... To be heard and believed, the gospel has to be proclaimed. ... Every Christian is to be a witness by word every time an occasion arises.

Suzanne de Dietrich,
French Reformed
lay theologian

Words never had it so good. They are used to inspire and inform movements, to start and encourage causes, to promote therapy, to engender love. Too bad that many believers have stopped believing in their potency.

Martin Marty,
Lutheran author,
critic, scholar

... Evangelism is the simple and pure telling of the Story. Those who make this point must be heard. They are reminding us of the "one-sidedness and naïvete of those who, mesmerized by secular Christianity, offer an "incognito evangelism of good works" as a substitute for story-telling.

Gabriel Fackre,
Professor, United
Church of Christ

### Futher Comment on Witness of Word

The New Testament provides us with some interesting examples of first century evangelism which may be suggestive for our word evangelism in this century.

Hans-Ruedi Weber of the World Council of Churches has pointed out that in the verse, "Always be prepared to make a defense to any one who calls you to account for the hope that is in you, yet do it with gentleness and reverence" (1 Peter 3:15), we have an old look at evangelism. In this text the picture is of the "outsider" questioning the "insider." The "outsider" wants to know how the Christian can live with such hope in the midst of a tragic world. As Peter recognized, such questions gave the Christians an opportunity to bear witness with "gentleness and reverence." The world still questions the church. If the congregation or Christian group of which we are a part manifests a radiant life of faith and hope and love, the world will ask us to explain the quality of our life. We then have a natural opportunity to witness to Christ, the source of all life. Often, questions addressed to the church today are like critical cross-examination. Even in responding to these questions with "gentleness and reverence," we find an opportunity to proclaim Christ. When the world begins the conversation we have a most natural occasion in which to speak of Christ.

In the book of Acts we read that Paul discussed "in the synagogue with the Jews and the devout persons and in the market place every day with those who chanced to be there" (Acts 17:17). The supermarket, the construction site, the bridge table, the business office, the garden club, the League of Women Voters, the classroom, the visit across the back fence, all of these provide possibilities for discussion of faith. Articles in the newspaper and popular books on religion may serve to spark a significant conversation. Alert and concerned Christians will find many occasions when they can start a discussion of the gospel.

Most frequently the method used in the New Testament is what might be called "the straightforward approach." Paul and other New Testament persons went to synagogues, market places, and homes with the sole purpose of telling about Christ. They raised the questions. They opened the discussion in terms of their message. Some modern day evangelism is impossibly subtle, circuitous, and non-directive by this New Testament directness. Today the church needs people who will seek "outsiders" and will unashamedly tell what they believe about Jesus Christ. When coupled with genuine respect for the persons to whom we are witnessing, the direct approach in evangelism will undoubtedly be as effective as it was in the first century.

No matter what approach we use in word evangelism we must be concerned to look beneath the surface of the life of the persons to whom we are talking. We must be willing to listen to their problems, questions, accusations, comments and excuses. We must identify with them in their deepest concerns. True evangelists recognize the real problems of the other person; they try to discover the elements of truth in the thinking of the other. At the right moment they have the courage to call the other person to faith in Christ.

**Congregations Are Multi-media**

We have discussed separately three aspects of congregational witness. In a living church these all flow together. Perhaps my own experience will illumine the way this happens:

Several years ago, as an amateur anthropologist, I set out to observe and learn about the life of two congregations in Cambridge, Massachusetts—Old Cambridge Baptist Church and First United Presbyterian Church. Careful notes were drawn from three Sunday services; conversations with individuals, and newsletters and bulletins were recorded. Old Cambridge Baptist Church would have to be termed *avant garde* in worship. Key words were "liberation" and "celebration." Concerns discussed included police brutality, McGovern's campaign, and the Third World. First Presbyterian was conservative and charismatic. Key words were "salvation" and "praise." Concerns discussed included Inter-Varsity in Boston, reaching out with the gospel to individuals, and a church center for senior citizens.

Despite these differences in style the two congregations had one main feature in common—an obvious and intensely warm feeling within the membership. This came to focus during Sunday morning worship when, in an informal time, the members talked freely of their hurts and worries, or told some good news. At the conclusion of this period of frank sharing, petitions and thanksgiving were offered to God. Though I had gone to these churches with an academic interest, I came away with an unintended by-product, a deeper trust in and stronger and broader loyalty to Christ and his cause. This "awakening" of my own faith through participation in these groups gave me a fresh glimpse of what may be happening to others who share in the life of a congregation.

Congregations—these and other ones—are multi-media. Communication takes place through symbolic action, color, music, emotion, service projects, all of this is a kind of background reinforcement for the verbal communication that is taking place. What was said to one another was a most influential part of the experience. (Language is perhaps *the* fundamental element in human community and communication.)

Gabriel Fackre has done more than anyone in recent years to remind the church that authentic evangelism must include all dimensions or else it foreshortens the biblical conception. In a recent article he reminds of this unity of witness in the life of our Lord:

> Jesus Christ spoke about the Kingdom of God in the midst of being and doing it. He preached and taught in the context of healing and serving. . . . At the center of the Christian story is no disembodied talk but the *Word made flesh*.[4]

The church as the body of Christ can do no less than the Master. The Apostle Peter seems to have had this wholeness of mission in mind when he wrote to the churches:

> Above all hold unfailing your love for one another, since love covers a multitude of sins. Practice hospitality ungrudgingly to one another. As each has received a gift, employ it for one another, as good stewards of God's varied grace: whoever speaks, as one who utters oracles of God; whoever renders service, as one who renders it by the strength which God supplies; in order that in everything God may be glorified through Jesus Christ. To him belong glory and dominion for ever and ever. Amen. (1 Peter 4:8–11).

The goal of every congregation must be that by good words and good works persons will come to glorify the Father through faith in Jesus Christ (Matthew 5:16).

## Congregations and Conversion

In recent decades some have learned to speak of the church in terms of "gathering" and "scattering," of "come-structures" and "go-structures." During these years the stress in witness has been on moving out beyond the four walls of the church building into the world. A classic statement of this position was written in the mid-fifties by the Department of the Laity of the World Council of Churches:

The real battles of faith today are being fought in factories, shops, offices, and farms, in political parties and government agencies, in countless homes, in the press, radio, and television, in the relationship of nations. Very often it is said that the church should go into these spheres; but the fact is that the church *is* already in these spheres in the persons of its laity.[5]

The extent to which our churches have reordered their lives by this thinking is remarkable, even if incomplete. The emphasis has been not only on individual presence but corporate as well. This world-centered orientation must continue. Nonetheless, as you can sense, we feel that the moment has come to reassert the valid and critically important emphasis on "coming in" and "gathering."

Our congregations aren't perfect, but they are places where, as Loren Mead said, persons get in touch with each other, the Scriptures, and God.

An invitation to come to church may be for someone the critical first step toward Christian faith. A person's values and world-view are determined most by the groups with which he/she closely associates. When warm hospitality is discovered, when friendship follows, when participation becomes frequent, then a person is in the best position to see, hear, and respond affirmatively to the Word of God.

Sociologist David Moberg's report on studies of conversion in *The Church as a Social Institution* bear on this point. He distinguishes two types of conversion:

1. *Ideological conversion*—persons change their minds and then seek fellowship with persons who share similar views.
2. *Reflexive conversion*—persons participate in a group, develop friendships and then change their minds to adopt at least some of the views of their associates.[6]

Of course, persons are converted in both ways. As a matter of fact, examples of both types are to be found in case studies scattered throughout this book. However, research indicates that more persons are converted in the second way. George E. Sweazey pointed to this fact when he wrote out of long pastoral experience: "Most Americans who are brought to faith today come along the growing edge of some congregation."[7] A young Ph.D. spoke of his "reflective conversion" in this way: "More than anything else it was the character of the congregation that led me to accept Christ."

**Conclusion**

Twenty years ago, in a volume of practical theology still worth reading, Charles D. Kean wrote words that first set me thinking about the manner in which the whole life of a congregation functions in evangelism:

If the local parish church is serving as an effective channel of the gospel, its total life is a reflection of God's saving act. . . . The local parish serves its purpose . . . by expressing the essential notes of the gospel—judgment, justification, sanctification—in its underlying philosophy, in its activities and in the structure through which these are related.[8]

The point we are making in this volume is similar. Given the gospel of God, the gathered life of God's people ought to reflect and transmit Christian faith.

How is the faith of persons who participate in your fellowship effected?

Is their faith increasingly drawn toward Jesus Christ and away from the various gods of culture?

Does their confidence in Christ grow stronger and their allegiance to him more steadfast?

Is their freedom to think and finally to say "yes" or "no" to Christ respected?

If so, your congregation may be said to have met through its witness of word, deed, and community life the criteria of the congregation in evangelism. These three criteria are:

1. A congregational life that transmits the centered character of the Christian faith.
2. A congregational life that transmits the relational character of the Christian faith.
3. A congregational life that transmits the personal character of the Christian faith.

It was once said of Pope John XXIII, "He made believing easier." To make believing easier for children growing up in the church and estranged-from-God adults outside its walls is the high calling of our congregations.

### FOR FURTHER REFLECTION

1. "The 'medium' of congregational life is the 'message.'" This sentence sums up the main point of this chapter. Taken quite literally, this means that the total life of a congregation—its way of receiving members, budget, sermons, service projects or lack thereof, worship services, women's activities, nursery attendants, salary for the sexton and secretary, church school, etc.—is a powerful communication network. Think of your own church. What is the message of your budget? What is the message of these other features of your church life? Does the Word made flesh in these aspects of your church life match up with the high sounding words your ministers and members speak in Sunday school and at worship? Do they complement or contradict each other?

2. The thought that evangelism has a threefold aspect—word, deed and life together—is derived from the Book of Acts, chapters 1 through 4. If you don't have time to read these chapters, you can review these verses: Acts 1:8; 2:44–47; 3:1–10; 4:8–12.

3. "The love of Christians for one another in the fellowship of the Christian community is evangelism." (John 13:34–35; John 17)
   a. Read over these Scripture references as well as those in number 2 above from the Book of Acts. What do they tell us about the witness made by our life together?
   b. Study the examples from the different centuries and different parts of the world in this section. From these, list several of the characteristics you would hope to see in any congregation.
   c. Propose some ways your church can make a more faithful witness by its community life.

4. "The lifestyle of the Christian person and the Christian community in radical obedience to the biblical mandates of the Kingdom of God in the world is evangelism." (Cf. Matthew 5:14–16; Matthew 25:31 ff.; Mark 12:29–31; Luke 4:16–21; John 20:21; Romans 12:1–2; Ephesians 3:10.)
   a. Read over these Scriptures. What do these tell us about "doing the Word"—the witness of deed?
   b. Again review the various examples and catalogue the various deeds to which they make reference.
   c. From your experience and observation, list some other examples of the witness of deed.
   d. How can you and your church group do a better job of practicing what is being preached in your pulpit?

5. "The proclamation of the Kingdom of God is evangelism." (Cf. Matthew 28:19–20; Mark 1:14–15; Luke 24:45–47; John 20–21; Romans 10:14–17; John 14:6.)
   a. Turn to these passages and read the words aloud.
   b. There is a chart in this chapter with four short quotations. Each deserves careful reflection and discussion. What is the main point they make?
   c. Grady Allison tells about a pastor in New York. Can you understand his problem? Why would he or any Christian have such a hang-up?
   d. How about your verbal witness? Your congregation's? What steps can be taken to overcome timidity? Brashness?

6. Is one of these three forms of evangelistic witness more important than another? Could one be ignored or dropped and the others be just as effective? If all are just moderately effective, does that stop God's work? If all are very effective, does that enhance the possibility of persons being won to Christ?

7. The aim of evangelism is conversion—this is a statement found early in chapter 1. At points along the way, you have found brief discussions of it. The material from David Molberg's book speaks of two types of conversion. Do you know persons who have come to Christ in each of these ways? How did the Apostle Paul come? Review some of the case studies in chapter 2. How did they? How did you come to Him?

8. Before you put the book down, flip back to the Table of Contents. Quickly review the journey you have taken through these pages. What are the three most helpful things you learned about evangelism? What personal commitment, if any, have you made as a result of this study? If you have been reading with a class, one last session could be held for the purpose of summing up and planning what you are going to do about evangelism and faith renewal in your church.

# Notes

## Chapter 1

1. David Stoner, "The Third Stage of Religion," *Faith at Work*, April, 1974, pp. 32–33.
2. Thomas Merton, *The Seven Storey Mountain* (New York: Harcourt, Brace & Co., 1948), pp. 108–110; reprinted in Mark Link, *He Is the Still Point of the Turning World* (Niles, Illinois: Argus Communications, 1971), p. 118.
3. Edith Black, "Rediscovery of Faith," *Radical Religion*, vol. I, no. 1, pp. 18–20.
4. Billy Graham, "The Hour of Decisions," in *Faith Is a Star* (New York: E. P. Dutton & Co., 1963), pp. 92–93.
5. F. Mallet-Jorris, "A Nativity Narrative," *Commonweal*, Dec. 27, 1968, pp. 92–93.
6. Agnes Campbell is a pseudonym for the person who submitted this account.
7. B. P. Dotsenko, "From Communism to Christianity," *Christianity Today*, Jan. 5, 1973, pp. 4–10.

## Chapter 2

1. *Time* Magazine, July 19, 1963, p. 80.
2. Quoted in H. Richard Niebuhr, *Radical Monotheism and Western Culture* (New York: Harper and Brothers, 1943, 1960), p. 20.
3. Eugene Kennedy, *Believing* (New York: Doubleday & Co., Inc., 1974), pp. 16–17.
4. Wilfred Cantrell Smith, *The Meaning and End of Religion* (New York: Mentor Books, 1962).
5. Cynthia Wedel, *Faith or Fear and Future Shock* (New York: Friendship Press, 1974).
6. *Ibid.*
7. Niebuhr, *op. cit.*
8. Paul Tillich, *Dynamics of Faith* (New York: Harper and Brothers, 1954), pp. 1–29.
(. Walter A. Brueggemann, "Empowered by Remembering and Hoping," *Evangelism for a New Day*, United Church of Christ, May, 1975, 1.
10. Niebuhr, *op. cit.*, pp. 17–18.
11. Robert Bellah, "Civil Religion and the Bicentennial," *Bicentennial Broadside* (New York: National Council of the Churches of Christ in the U.S.A., 1975), p. 6.
12. Mark Hatfield, *Faith at Work*, August, 1971, p. 10.
13. Quoted in the *Houston Chronicle, New York Times* News Service, December 19, 1975.

## Chapter 3

1. Rudolph Bultmann, "Pistis," *Kittel's Theological Dictionary of the New Testament* (Grand Rapids: Eerdmans), vol. VI, pp. 119, 225.

2. Rose Kennedy, *Times to Remember* (Garden City: Doubleday & Co., 1974), p. 520.
3. J. Jeremias, The Prayers of Jesus (Napierville, Ill.: Alec R. Allenson, Inc., 1967), p. 62.
4. *Niebuhr, op. cit.*, p. 18.
5. Hans-Ruedi Weber, *The Militant Ministry* (Philadelphia: Fortress Press, 1967), pp. 1–4.
6. George Sherwood Eddy, *Religion and Social Justice* (New York: George H. Doran & Co., 1927), p. 196f.
7. Dietrich Bonhoeffer, *The Cost of Discipleship* (New York: the Macmillan Co., rev. ed. 1949), p. 36f.
8. John Wesley, *The Journal of The Rev. John Wesley, A.M.* (London: J. Kershaw, 1827), vol. I, pp. 90–91.

**Chapter 4**
1. C. S. Lewis, *Surprised by Joy* (New York: Harcourt, Brace & Co., 1955), p. 224.
2. Robert Frost, *Collected Poems of Robert Frost* (Garden City: Doubleday & Co., 1942), p. 131.
3. Barry Chazan, "Indoctrination and Religious Education," *Religious Education*, July-August, 1972, pp. 243–52.
4. Gordon Allport, *Becoming* (New Haven: Yale University Press, 1955), pp. 33–55.
5. Frost, *op. cit.*
6. From *Youth* Magazine; quoted in Mark Link, *He Is the Still Point of the Turning World* (Niles, Ill.: Argus Communications, 1971), p. 28.
7. Byron Knight and Herman Ahrens, "Billy Graham: A Personal Conversation," *Youth* Magazine, March, 1975, p. 75.

**Chapter 5**
1. Professor James Fowler of the Divinity School, Harvard University, hypothesizes that there are stages of faith development. His system incorporates insights from Erikson, Piaget, and Lawrence Kohlberg on moral development and H. Richard Niebuhr. Fowler's theory is now being subjected to empirical testing. His system, while immensely complex, has some large implications for training pastors and others who are concerned about preaching, education, counseling, and evangelism. It was my good fortune to receive a Merrill Fellowship to the Divinity School in the fall of 1972. During that time my study was concentrated with Professors Fowler and Kohlberg. In this chapter I do not argue that there are stages of faith or moral development, as they do. Instead, I am taking the simpler, more cautious approach of setting forth styles of faithing that seem to be present at different ages during our human pilgrimage. It was Professor Fowler who first opened my eyes to this and then provided for me the context within which to affirm it.
2. Of the many writings by Erikson, the following, all published by W. W. Norton and Co., New York, and readily available in paperback, are pertinent to our discussion: 1. *Childhood and Society*, 1950; 2. *Young Man Luther*, 1958; 3. *Insight and Responsibility*, 1964; 4. *Identity: Youth and Crisis*, 1968.
3. Erik Erikson, "Growth and Crises of the Healthy Personality," xerox copy, Andover Library, Harvard University, p. 65.

4. Ronald Goldman, *Religious Thinking from Childhood to Adolescence* (New York: Seabury Press, 1964), p. 231.
5. Paul Tillich, *On the Boundary Line* (New York: Charles Scribner's Sons, 1966), p. 14.
6. Johanna K. Link, *Your Child and Religion* (Richmond: John Knox Press, 1972), p. 224.
7. Goldman, *op. cit.*, p. 234.
8. Rose Kennedy, *loc. cit.*
9. *Young Man Luther*, p. 110.
10. *Identity: Youth and Crisis*, pp. 186–87.
11. Richard I. Evans, *Dialogue with Erik Erikson* (N.Y.: E. P. Dutton & Co., 1969), p. 30.
12. *Identity: Youth and Crisis*, p. 35.
13. *Ibid.*, p. 30.
14. Edward R. Murrow, ed., *This I Believe* (New York: Simon & Schuster, 1954).
15. Lloyd J. Averill, *Between Faith and Unfaith* (Richmond: John Knox Press, 1967), p. 24.
16. Merton P. Strommen, *Five Cries of Youth* (New York: Harper & Row, 1974), pp. 122–25.
17. John Westerhoff, III, "Church Education for Tomorrow," *Christian Century*, Dec. 31, 1975, p. 1203.

**Chapter 6**

1. Adapted from Sam Shoemaker, *Extraordinary Living for Ordinary Men* (Grand Rapids: Zondervan, 1965), pp. 158–60.
2. Wilfred Cantrell Smith, *op. cit.*, p. 309.
3. *Ibid.*, p. 141.
$. Loren Mead, "Evangelism: Notes Toward a Better Understanding." Occasional paper, mimeographed, Board of National Ministries, Presbyterian Church, U.S., pp. 3–5.
5. The Proposed New Confession of Faith, Presbyterian Church, U.S., 1972, VIII, 5.
6. Martin E. Marty, "Both Personal Commitment and Social Concern," *Presbyterian Outlook*, January 15, 1973, pp. 5–6.
7. Robert F. Ball, sermon on faith preached at Memorial Drive Presbyterian Church, Houston, Texas, 1974.

**Chapter 7**

1. Loren Mead and James D. Anderson, "Why Bother With Parishes?", Catacomb Cassettes, 15 16th St., Atlanta, Georgia 30309.
2. "How Organizations Function," *Strengthening the Local Church*, Council for Lay Life and Work, United Church of Christ, N.Y., mimeographed, pp. 1–11. For a further and more adequate discussion of the inner dynamics of congregational life, the reader is referred to this and other insightful materials of the U.C.C.
3. George E. Sweazey, "A Call for Spiritual Intensity," *Presbyterian Outlook*, Dec. 7, 1970, p. 6.
4. Peter Berger, "A Call for Authority in the Christian Community," Christian Century, October 27, 1971, p. 126f.

**Chapter 8**
1. Eugene Kennedy, *op. cit.,* p. 187.
2. Harvey Cox, *The Seduction of the Spirit* (New York: Simon & Schuster, 1973), p. 52.
3. James Gustafson, "Religiosity—An Irritating Necessity," *Christianity and Crisis,* 1962.
4. Gabriel Fackre, "Evangelism: Meaning, Context, Mandate," *The Christian Ministry,* March, 1973.
5. World Council of Churches, *The Ministry of the Laity in the World,* a statement commended to the churches for their study and comment (Geneva: World Council of Churches, 1956).
6. David Moberg, *The Church as a Social Institution* (Englewood Cliffs, N.J.: Prentice-Hall, 1962), p. 426.
7. Sweazey, *op. cit.*
8. C. D. Kean, *The Christian Gospel and the Parish Church* (New York: Seabury Press, 1953), pp. 4–5.